Redundant

Leo Butler

Methuen Drama

Methuen Drama

1 3 5 7 9 10 8 6 4 2

Published in Great Britain in 2001 by
Methuen Publishing Limited

A CIP catalogue record for this book is available from the British
Library

ISBN 0 413 77169 5

Typeset by SX Composing DTP, Rayleigh, Essex
Printed and bound in Great Britain by
Cox & Wyman Ltd, Reading, Berkshir

Caution

ROYAL COURT

Royal Court Theatre presents

REDUNDANT

by **Leo Butler**

First performance at the Royal Court Jerwood Theatre Downstairs,
Sloane Square, London on 6 September 2001.

Supported by Jerwood New Playwrights.

REDUNDANT

by **Leo Butler**

Cast in order of appearance
Lucy **Lyndsey Marshal**
Darren **Simon Trinder**
Dave **Wil Johnson**
Gonzo **Craig Heaney**
Nikki **Rachel Brogan**
Jo **Eileen O'Brien**

Director **Dominic Cooke**
Designer **Robert Innes Hopkins**
Lighting Designer **Peter Mumford**
Sound Designer **Gareth Fry**
Composer **Gary Yershon**
Assistant Director **Joseph Hill-Gibbins**
Casting Director **Lisa Makin**
Production Manager **Paul Handley**
Company Stage Manager **Cath Binks**
Stage Manager **Fiona Greenhill**
Deputy Stage Manager **Rachael Claire Lovett**
Assistant Stage Manager **Kala Simpson**
Costume Supervisor **Suzanne Duffy**
Fight Director **Terry King**
Dialects **Penny Dyer**
Company Voice Work **Patsy Rodenburg**

Royal Court Theatre would like to thank the following for their help with this production:
Wardrobe care by Persil and Comfort courtesy of Lever Faberge.

THE COMPANY

Leo Butler (writer)
For the Royal Court: Made of Stone (Exposure, Young Writers' Festival, 2000).
Television: Jerusalem the Golden (BBC Fictionlab).
Awards include: Peggy Ramsay Foundation Award for Individual Writing (1999) and the George Devine Award for Redundant (2001).

Rachel Brogan
Theatre includes: Road (Contact, Manchester).
Television includes: Child's Play, Cool Cube.

Dominic Cooke (director)
Associate Director of the Royal Court.
For the Royal Court: Spinning Into Butter, Fireface, Other People.
Other theatre includes: As adapter and director: Arabian Nights (Young Vic/UK and world tour/New Victory Theatre, New York); The Marriage of Figaro (tour). As director: Hunting Scenes From Lower Bavaria, The Weavers (Gate), Afore Night Come, Entertaining Mr Sloane (Theatr Clwyd); Bullet (Donmar Warehouse); My Mother Said I Never Should (Oxford Stage Company/ Young Vic); Of Mice and Men (Nottingham Playhouse); Kiss Of the Spiderwoman (Bolton Octagon); Autogeddon (Edinburgh Assembly Rooms); Caravan (National Theatre of Norway); The Importance of Being Earnest (Atlantic Theatre Festival, Canada).
Opera includes: I Capuleti e i Montacchi (Grange Park Opera).
Awards include: TMA Theatre Award for Arabian Nights, Manchester Evening News Drama Award for the Marriage of Figaro and Edinburgh Fringe First for Autogeddon.
Assistant Director at the Royal Shakespeare Company 1992-94.

Gareth Fry (sound designer)
For the Royal Court: Mountain Language & Ashes To Ashes, The Country.
Other theatre includes: The Oresteia (RNT); Noise of Time, Mnemonic, The Street of Crocodiles (Theatre de Complicite); Wexford Trilogy (Oxford Stage Company); Play to Win (Soho Theatre & national tour).

Craig Heaney
Theatre includes: Charley's Aunt (Etcetera Theatre); Stags and Hens (Canal Café); Blood Sweat and Tears (Bedlam, Edinburgh); The Rink (Southside, Edinburgh); A Midsummer Night's Dream (Trent Park) The Dumb Waiter, In to the Woods, Pirates of Penzance (Simmonds Theatre); Twist and Shout (European tour); Great Pretenders (Gilded Balloon, Edinburgh); Chicago (Forum).
Television includes: Breeze Block, Staying Up, Band of Brothers, Grange Hill, Peak Practice, Badger, Dangerfield, Casualty, Cone Zone, The Bill, King Leek, Our Friends in the North.
Film includes: Out of Depth, Mild and Bitter.

Joseph Hill-Gibbins (assistant director)
For the Royal Court as assistant director: Blasted, Spinning Into Butter.
As assistant director, theatre includes: Hobson's Choice (Stephen Joseph Theatre, Scarborough); Corpse (Haymarket, Basingstoke); Woyzeck (Didsbury Studio, Manchester).
As director, theatre includes: The Lonesome West (Manchester University); The Dark (also co-wrote), Rat In The Skull (Edinburgh Fringe).
Joseph is also a senior script reader at the Royal Court and a member of the Young Writers' Programme.
Joseph is the recipient of the Rose Bruford Memorial Trust Director's Award 2001.

Robert Innes Hopkins (designer)
For the Royal Court: Other People.
Other theatre includes: The Villain's Opera, Romeo and Juliet (RNT); The Servant of Two Masters, Comedy of Errors (RSC); Les Miserables (Tel Aviv Arts Centre); The Tempest, Present Laughter, The Seagull, The Wasp Factory (West Yorkshire Playhouse); Othello (Washington Shakespeare Theatre); My Mother Said I Never Should (Oxford Stage Company/Tour); The Weavers, Hunting Scenes From Lower Bavaria, Fatzer Material (Gate Theatre); Imperfect Librarian, Spell, Hunger (Young Vic Studio); Happy End (Nottingham Playhouse); Miss Julie (Young Vic); Judith (Wrestling School).
Film includes: Lucia Di Lammermoor.
Opera includes: Wozzeck (Santa Fé Opera); I Capuleti e i Montecchi (Grange Park Opera); Paradise Moscow, The Elixir of Love, The Bartered Bride (Opera North); Mr Emmet Takes a Walk (Orkney Festival).
Awards include: Critics' Circle Designer of the Year 1996 for The Weavers and Comedy of Errors. TMA Designer of the Year 1997 for The Wasp Factory and My Mother Said I Never Should.

Wil Johnson

Theatre includes: A Mad World My Masters, As You like It (Globe); The Taming of the Shrew, A Midsummer Night's Dream (Southern Shakespeare Festival); Pow! (Paines Plough tour); Blood Knot (Gate); The Queen and I (Vaudeville); Running Dream (Stratford East); The Snow Queen (Young Vic); Back up the Hearse (Hampstead); Cinderella (West Yorkshire Playhouse); My Children, My Africa (Harrogate); Macbeth (RNT Studio tour); Sir Thomas More (Shaw Theatre); Sugar Hill (US tour); Fuente Ovejuna (RNT); The Bacchae (Shared Experience); Fire, Black Poppies, Macbeth Rhapsody in Black'n'White, Shakespeare in Dialect (RNT Studio); Thriller (Oval House); Revo (Umoja Theatre Company); Waiting for Hannibal (Black Theatre Co-op); Noah's Wife (Traverse); Skin Deep (Tyne & Wear Theatre Co.); Four Seasons (Albany Empire); Twelfth Night (Zimbabwe tour).

Television includes: Babyfather, Waking the Dead, Buried Treasure, Clocking Off, A Midsummer Night's Dream, Cracker, The Felix Dexter Show, The Bill, White Goods, Mr Don & Mr George, Crime Ltd, Alexi Sayle Show, Teaching Matthew, Anna Lee, Rides, Look at It This Way, Starting Out, In the Pink, Home-Front, London's Burning, Casualty.

Film includes: South West Nine, Native, Emotional Backgammon, Babymother, Midnight Breaks, Secrets.

Lyndsey Marshal

For the Royal Court: Fireface.

Other theatre includes: Boston Marriage (Donmar); Top Girls (New Vic); Miss Julie (Caird Studio and tour); The Maids (Venue 13, Edinburgh); Our Country's Good (Library Theatre).

Television includes: That's Not Me, Peak Practice, Midsomer Murders.

Film includes: The Hours.

Radio includes: Tess of the D'Urbevilles.

Peter Mumford (lighting designer)

Theatre includes: Hamlet, Othello, The Taming of the Shrew (RSC); Iphigenia (Abbey, Dublin); God Only Knows (Vaudeville); Medea (Queen's); The Dispute & The Critic (Royal Exchange, Manchester); Lautrec (Shaftesbury); Summerfolk, The Merchant of Venice, Money, The Prime of Miss Jean Brodie (RNT); A Long Day's Journey into Night, An Ideal Husband, Oliver Twist, Therese Raquin (Gate, Dublin).

Opera includes: Earth and the Great Weather (also directed, Almeida Opera 2000); Un Ballo In Maschera (Vilinius Festival); Don Pasquale (Opera Zuid, Holland); The Coronation of Poppaea (ENO); Eugene Onegin, Madame Butterfly (Opera North); Guilio Cesare (Opera de Bordeaux).

Dance includes: Of Oil and Water (Siobhan Davies Dance Co.); Irek Mukhamedov and Dancers (Sadler's Wells); Arthur (Birmingham Royal Ballet); The Crucible, Hidden Variables, A Stranger's Taste, This House Will Burn (Royal Ballet); Sounding the Celebrated Soubrette (Rambert Dance Co.).

Peter won the Laurence Olivier Award for Outstanding Achievement in Dance for The Glass Blew In and Fearful Symmetries and was nominated for Best Lighting Designer in 2000.

Eileen O'Brien

For the Royal Court: The Knocky.

Other theatre includes: Death of a Salesman (Manchester Library); A Doll's House (Shared Experience); Prize Night, The Plough and The Stars (Manchester Royal Exchange); Enjoy (West Yorkshire Playhouse); Richard III (Northern Broadsides); Derby Day, Stop the Children's Laughter (Bolton Octagon); Funny Peculiar (Garrick); Absent Friends, Bedroom Farce, Confusions (Theatre in the Round, Scarborough); Breezeblock Park (Liverpool Everyman); A Doll's House, Alfie (Liverpool Playhouse); The Caucasian Chalk Circle (Manchester Contact).

Television includes: Mersey Beat, Casualty, The Vice, The Life and Crimes of William Palmer, Brookside, And the Beat Goes On, No Bananas, The Life and Times of Henry Pratt, Rockcliffe's Babies, The Nation's Health, Boys from the Blackstuff, How We Used To Live, Eastenders, The Practice, The Sheikh of Pickersgill, One in a Thousand, The Last Company Car, The Crezz, The Adventures of Sherlock Holmes, Chillers, Hearts and Minds, The Bill, A Touch of Frost, Last of the Summer Wine.

Film includes: A Private Function, Runners, A Month in The Country, Between Two Women, Fanny and Elvis.

Radio includes: Red Rock, Grey Rock, The Monument.

Simon Trinder
Theatre includes: Buried Alive (Hampstead);
Black and White (New Vic Borderlines); The
World Turned Upside Down (Sherman Theatre,
Cardiff); Golden Swords (Globe); The Maids
(Edinburgh Fringe); Kes (Bolton Octagon).
Television includes: Electric Chair.
Film includes: The Pros, The Cons and a Screw.
Radio includes: Electricity, The Man Who Came
to Dinner, Smelling of Roses.
Simon was the recipient of the BBC Carleton
Hobbs Bursary Award 2000.

Gary Yershon (composer)
For the Royal Court: Fireface, Hysteria,
Inventing a New Colour.
Other theatre includes: Boston Marriage
(Donmar); A Doll's House (Shared Experience);
Twelfth Night, The Rivals, The Taming of the
Shrew, Don Carlos, Hamlet, The Unexpected
Man, As You Like It, The Merchant of Venice,
Artists and Admirers, The Virtuoso (RSC); Life x
3, Further Than the Furthest Thing, Widowers'
Houses, Troilus and Cressida, The Way of the
World, The Tempest, Broken Glass, Pericles
(RNT); Marathon, Hunting Scenes from Lower
Bavaria, The Weavers (Gate); Arabian Nights,
Miss Julie (Young Vic); Peter Pan, The
Government Inspector, A Perfect Ganesh, Death
of a Salesman, The Hypochondriac, Don Juan
(West Yorkshire Playhouse); Art (Wyndham's
Theatre/New York); Rosita the Spinster
(Almeida); Medea, The School for Scandal,
Tartuffe, Julius Caesar, The Winter's Tale
(Manchester Royal Exchange).
Television includes: Painted Tales, James the Cat.
Film includes: Topsy-Turvy.
Radio includes: Ruslan and Lyudmila, The
Wasting Game, In the Solitude of the Cotton
Fields, Room of Leaves.

THE ENGLISH STAGE COMPANY AT THE ROYAL COURT

The English Stage Company at the Royal Court opened in 1956 as a subsidised theatre producing new British plays, international plays and some classical revivals.

The first artistic director George Devine aimed to create a writers' theatre, 'a place where the dramatist is acknowledged as the fundamental creative force in the theatre and where the play is more important than the actors, the director, the designer'. The urgent need was to find a contemporary style in which the play, the acting, direction and design are all combined. He believed that 'the battle will be a long one to continue to create the right conditions for writers to work in'.

Devine aimed to discover 'hard-hitting, uncompromising writers whose plays are stimulating, provocative and exciting'. The Royal Court production of John Osborne's Look Back in Anger in May 1956 is now seen as the decisive starting point of modern British drama and the policy created a new generation of British playwrights. The first wave included John Osborne, Arnold Wesker, John Arden, Ann Jellicoe, N F Simpson and Edward Bond. Early seasons included new international plays by Bertolt Brecht, Eugène Ionesco, Samuel Beckett, Jean-Paul Sartre and Marguerite Duras.

The theatre started with the 400-seat proscenium arch Theatre Downstairs, and then in 1969 opened a second theatre, the 60-seat studio Theatre Upstairs. Some productions transfer to the West End, such as Caryl Churchill's Far Away, Conor McPherson's The Weir, Kevin Elyot's Mouth to Mouth and My Night With Reg. The Royal Court also co-produces plays which have transferred to the West End or toured internationally, such as Sebastian Barry's The Steward of Christendom and Mark Ravenhill's Shopping and Fucking (with Out of Joint), Martin McDonagh's The Beauty Queen Of Leenane (with Druid Theatre Company), Ayub Khan-Din's East is East (with Tamasha Theatre Company, and now a feature film).

Since 1994 the Royal Court's artistic policy has again been vigorously directed to finding and producing a new generation of playwrights. The writers include Joe Penhall, Rebecca Prichard, Michael Wynne, Nick Grosso, Judy Upton, Meredith Oakes, Sarah Kane, Anthony Neilson, Judith Johnson, James Stock, Jez Butterworth, Marina Carr, Simon Block, Martin McDonagh, Mark Ravenhill, Ayub Khan-Din, Tamantha Hammerschlag, Jess Walters, Che Walker, Conor McPherson, Simon Stephens, Richard Bean, Roy

photo: Andy Chopping

Williams, Gary Mitchell, Mick Mahoney, Rebecca Gilman, Christopher Shinn, Kia Corthron, David Gieselmann, Marius von Mayenburg and David Eldridge. This expanded programme of new plays has been made possible through the support of A.S.K Theater Projects, the Jerwood Charitable Foundation, the American Friends of the Royal Court Theatre and many in association with the Royal National Theatre Studio.

In recent years there have been record-breaking productions at the box office, with capacity houses for Jez Butterworth's Mojo, Sebastian Barry's The Steward of Christendom, Martin McDonagh's The Beauty Queen of Leenane, Ayub Khan-Din's East is East, Eugène Ionesco's The Chairs, David Hare's My Zinc Bed and Conor McPherson's The Weir, which transferred to the West End in October 1998 and ran for nearly two years at the Duke of York's Theatre.

The newly refurbished theatre in Sloane Square opened in February 2000, with a policy still inspired by the first artistic director George Devine. The Royal Court is an international theatre for new plays and new playwrights, and the work shapes contemporary drama in Britain and overseas.

AWARDS FOR
THE ROYAL COURT

Terry Johnson's Hysteria won the 1994 Olivier Award for Best Comedy, and also the Writers' Guild Award for Best West End Play. Kevin Elyot's My Night with Reg won the 1994 Writers' Guild Award for Best Fringe Play, the Evening Standard Award for Best Comedy, and the 1994 Olivier Award for Best Comedy. Joe Penhall was joint winner of the 1994 John Whiting Award for Some Voices. Sebastian Barry won the 1995 Writers' Guild Award for Best Fringe Play, the 1995 Critics' Circle Award and the 1997 Christopher Ewart-Biggs Literary Prize for The Steward of Christendom, and the 1995 Lloyds Private Banking Playwright of the Year Award. Jez Butterworth won the 1995 George Devine Award for Most Promising Playwright, the 1995 Writers' Guild New Writer of the Year Award, the Evening Standard Award for Most Promising Playwright and the 1995 Olivier Award for Best Comedy for Mojo.

The Royal Court won the 1995 Prudential Award for Theatre and was the overall winner of the 1995 Prudential Award for the Arts for creativity, excellence, innovation and accessibility. The Royal Court Theatre Upstairs won the 1995 Peter Brook Empty Space Award for innovation and excellence in theatre.

Michael Wynne won the 1996 Meyer-Whitworth Award for The Knocky. Martin McDonagh won the 1996 George Devine Award, the 1996 Writers' Guild Best Fringe Play Award, the 1996 Critics' Circle Award and the 1996 Evening Standard Award for Most Promising Playwright for The Beauty Queen of Leenane. Marina Carr won the 19th Susan Smith Blackburn Prize (1996/7) for Portia Coughlan. Conor McPherson won the 1997 George Devine Award, the 1997 Critics' Circle Award and the 1997 Evening Standard Award for Most Promising Playwright for The Weir. Ayub Khan-Din won the 1997 Writers' Guild Award for Best West End Play, the 1997 Writers' Guild New Writer of the Year Award and the 1996 John Whiting Award for East is East. Anthony Neilson won the 1997 Writers' Guild Award for Best Fringe Play for The Censor.

At the 1998 Tony Awards, Martin McDonagh's The Beauty Queen of Leenane (co-production with Druid Theatre Company) won four awards including Garry Hynes for Best Director and was nominated for a further two. Eugene Ionesco's The Chairs (co-production with Theatre de Complicite) was nominated for six Tony awards. David Hare won the 1998 Time Out Live Award for Outstanding Achievement and six awards in New York including the Drama League, Drama Desk and New York Critics Circle Award for Via Dolorosa. Sarah Kane won the 1998 Arts Foundation Fellowship in Playwriting. Rebecca Prichard won the 1998 Critics' Circle Award for Most Promising Playwright for Yard Gal (co-production with Clean Break).

Conor McPherson won the 1999 Olivier Award for Best New Play for The Weir. The Royal Court won the 1999 ITI Award for Excellence in International Theatre. Sarah Kane's Cleansed was judged Best Foreign Language Play in 1999 by Theater Heute in Germany. Gary Mitchell won the 1999 Pearson Best Play Award for Trust. Rebecca Gilman was joint winner of the 1999 George Devine Award and won the 1999 Evening Standard Award for Most Promising Playwright for The Glory of Living.

Roy Williams and Gary Mitchell were joint winners of the George Devine Award 2000 for Most Promising Playwright for Lift Off and The Force of Change respectively. At the Barclays Theatre Awards 2000 presented by the TMA, Richard Wilson won the Best Director Award for David Gieselmann's Mr Kolpert and Jeremy Herbert won the Best Designer Award for Sarah Kane's 4.48 Psychosis. Gary Mitchell won the Evening Standard's Charles Wintour Award 2000 for Most Promising Playwright for The Force of Change. Stephen Jeffreys' I Just Stopped by to See The Man won an AT&T: On Stage Award 2000. David Eldridge's Under the Blue Sky won the Time Out Live Award 2001 for Best New Play in the West End.

In 1999, the Royal Court won the European theatre prize New Theatrical Realities, presented at Taormina Arte in Sicily, for its efforts in recent years in discovering and producing the work of young British dramatists.

ROYAL COURT BOOKSHOP

The bookshop offers a wide range of playtexts, theatre books, screenplays and art-house videos with over 1,000 titles. Located in the downstairs Bar and Food area, the bookshop is open Monday to Saturday, afternoons and evenings.

Many Royal Court playtexts are available for just £2 including the plays in the current season and recent works by David Hare, Conor McPherson, Martin Crimp, Sarah Kane, David Mamet, Gary Mitchell, Martin McDonagh, Ayub Khan-Din, Jim Cartwright and Rebecca Prichard. We offer a 10% reduction to students on a range of titles.
Further information : 020 7565 5024

REBUILDING THE ROYAL COURT

In 1995, the Royal Court was awarded a National Lottery grant through the Arts Council of England, to pay for three quarters of a £26m project to completely rebuild its 100-year old home. The rules of the award required the Royal Court to raise £7.6m in partnership funding. The building has been completed thanks to the generous support of those listed below.

We are particularly grateful for the contributions of over 5,700 audience members.

English Stage Company Registered Charity number 231242.

ROYAL COURT DEVELOPMENT BOARD
Tamara Ingram (Chair)
Jonathan Cameron (Vice Chair)
Timothy Burrill
Anthony Burton
Jonathan Caplan QC
Deborah Davis
Cecily Engle
Julia Hobsbawm
Joyce Hytner
Mary Ellen Johnson
Dan Klein
Michael Potter
Mark Robinson
William Russell
Sue Stapely

PRINCIPAL DONOR
Jerwood Foundation

WRITERS CIRCLE
The Cadogan Estate
Carillon/Schal
News International plc
Pathé
The Eva and Hans K Rausing Trust
The Rayne Foundation
Sky
Garfield Weston Foundation

DIRECTORS CIRCLE
The Esmée Fairbairn Foundation
The Granada Group plc

ACTORS CIRCLE
Edwin C Cohen & The Blessing Way Foundation
Ronald Cohen & Sharon Harel-Cohen
Quercus Charitable Trust
The Basil Samuel Charitable Trust
The Trusthouse Charitable Foundation
The Woodward Charitable Trust

SPECIFIC DONATIONS
The Foundation for Sport and the Arts for Stage System
John Lewis Partnership plc for Balcony
City Parochial Foundation for Infra Red Induction Loops and Toilets for Disabled Patrons
RSA Art for Architecture Award Scheme for Antoni Malinowski Wall Painting

THE AMERICAN FRIENDS OF THE ROYAL COURT THEATRE

AFRCT support the mission of the Royal Court and are primarily focused on raising funds to enable the theatre to produce new work by emerging American writers. Since this not-for-profit organisation was founded in 1997, AFRCT has contributed to seven productions including Rebecca Gilman's Spinning Into Butter. They have also supported the participation of young artists in the Royal Court's acclaimed International Residency.

If you would like to support the ongoing work of the Royal Court, please contact the Development Department on 020 7565 5050.

AMERICAN FRIENDS

Founders
Harry Brown
Victoria Elenowitz
Francis Finlay
Monica Gerard-Sharp
The Howard Gilman Foundation
Jeananne Hauswald
Mary Ellen Johnson
Dany Khosrovani
Kay Koplovitz
The Laura Pels Foundation
Stephen Magowan
Monica Menell-Kinberg Ph.D.
Benjamin Rauch
Rory Riggs
Robert Rosenkranz
Gerald Schoenfeld, The Shubert Organization

Patrons
Daniel Baudendistel
Arthur Bellinzoni
Miriam Bienstock
Robert L & Janice Billingsley
Catherine G Curran
Leni Darrow
Michael & Linda Donovan
Ursula & William Fairbairn
April Foley
Amanda Foreman
Mr & Mrs Richard Gelfond
Mr & Mrs Richard Grand
Mr & Mrs Paul Hallingby
Sharon King Hoge
The Carl C Icahn Family Foundation
Maurice & Jean R Jacobs
Mr & Mrs Ernest Kafka
Sahra T Lese
Susan & Martin Lipton
Eleanor Margolis

Hamish & Georgone Maxwell
Kathleen O'Grady
Howard & Barbara Sloan
Margaret Jackson Smith
Mika Sterling
Arielle Tepper
The Thorne Foundation

Benefactors
Mr & Mrs Tom Armstrong
Mr & Mrs Mark Arnold
Elaine Attias
Rachael Bail
Mr & Mrs Matthew Chapman
David Day
Richard & Rosalind Edelman
Abe & Florence Elenowitz
Hiram & Barbara Gordon
Mr & Mrs Brian Keelan
Jennifer C E Laing
Burt Lerner
Imelda Liddiard
Dr Anne Locksley
Mr & Mrs Rudolph Rauch
Lawrence & Helen Remmel
Mr & Mrs Robert Rosenberg
Mr & Mrs William Russell
Harold Sanditen
Mr & Mrs Robert Scully
Julie Talen
Mr & Mrs Charles Whitman

ARTS COUNCIL OF ENGLAND

PROGRAMME SUPPORTERS

The Royal Court (English Stage Company Ltd) receives its principal funding from London Arts. It is also supported financially by a wide range of private companies and public bodies and earns the remainder of its income from the box office and its own trading activities.

The Royal Borough of Kensington & Chelsea gives an annual grant to the Royal Court Young Writers' Programme and the London Boroughs Grants Committee provides project funding for a number of play development initiatives.

The Jerwood Charitable Foundation continues to support new plays by new playwrights through the Jerwood New Playwrights series. Since 1993 the A.S.K. Theater Projects of Los Angeles has funded a Playwrights' Programme at the theatre. Bloomberg Mondays, the Royal Court's reduced price ticket scheme, is supported by Bloomberg.

LONDON ARTS

JERWOOD
NEW PLAYWRIGHTS

Since 1993 Jerwood New Playwrights have contributed to some of the Royal Court's most successful productions, including SHOPPING AND FUCKING by Mark Ravenhill (co-production with Out of Joint), EAST IS EAST by Ayub Khan-Din (co-production with Tamasha), THE BEAUTY QUEEN OF LEENANE by Martin McDonagh (co-production with Druid Theatre Company), THE WEIR by Conor McPherson, REAL CLASSY AFFAIR by Nick Grosso, THE FORCE OF CHANGE by Gary Mitchell, ON RAFTERY'S HILL by Marina Carr (co-production with Druid Theatre Company), 4.48 PSYCHOSIS by Sarah Kane, UNDER THE BLUE SKY by David Eldridge, PRESENCE by David Harrower, HERONS by Simon Stephens and CLUBLAND by Roy Williams.

The Jerwood Charitable Foundation is a registered charity dedicated to imaginative and responsible funding and sponsorship of the arts, education, design and other areas of human endeavour and excellence. This season Jerwood New Playwrights are supporting REDUNDANT by Leo Butler, NIGHTINGALE AND CHASE by Zinnie Harris and F***ING GAMES by Grae Cleugh.

HERONS by Simon Stephens
(photo: Pete Jones)

EAST IS EAST by Ayub Khan-Din
(photo: Robert Day)

Redundant

For Mum, Dad and Matt

'No matter. Try again. Fail again. Fail better.'

                                   – Samuel Beckett

Characters:

Lucy, 17 years old, white.
Darren, 17 years old, black.
Nikki, 16 years, Lucy's sister, mixed race.
Dave, 32 years old, black.
Gonzo, 23 years, white.
Jo, 60 years, Lucy's gran, white.

Setting:

Sheffield. Between December 1999 and December 2000.

Lucy's council flat, third/top floor. Lounge/Bedroom.
Front door, leading to stairway. Alcove leading to bathroom
and a kitchen. One window with curtains. Grotty double
bed, near the window. Small old portable television. Small
tapedeck. Box of tapes. No telephone. No carpet. Floor is
covered with lino. Old chest of drawers, stuffed with clothes.
On top of the chest are cosmetics and cheap jewellry, a
small mirror and a small framed photo of a toddler. Damp
yellow walls. Poster of Bob Marley. Old electric heater fitted
into the wall. Some kind of seating: cushions, beanbags, the
odd crappy chair perhaps. The flat should be cluttered with
clothes and various junk.

The writer would like to acknowledge Graham Whybrow,
Ian Rickson, Dominic Cooke, Simon Stephens and, most
importantly, Ola Animashawun, with everyone at the YWP,
for their support and guidance in the writing of this play.

Scene One

Night. December.
The heater is off.
Lucy *stands by the window, looking out.*
Darren *sits on the sofa, eating chips and battered sausage with his hands.*

Lucy   Reckon it'll snow this year?

Pause.

Lucy   Can't 'member last time it snowed.

Darren   Too wet f'snow. Evaporates on its way down like.

Lucy   All smog n'that?

Darren   Yeah.

Lucy   I know. Not like when we wa' kids. Did yer ever go sledgin' or owt?

Darren   Oh aye, all time. Just over down whatsit, Ecclesall Park n'that. Loads en'us on plastic bags bombin' it down 'ill. Used t'love it. Snow fights, sledgin'.

Lucy   Ever build a snowman?

Darren   Oh aye.

Lucy   No yer never. Only girls build snowmen.

Darren   Eh?

Lucy   Only girls build snowmen.

Darren   Naow.

Lucy   Must be a puff. Uuuuuur.

Darren   Naow, only when I were little. Wi'me sisters n'that.

Lucy   I jus' like watchin' it me. Like the way it covers everythin' up, so yer can't tell what's what.

Pause. She shuts the curtains.

You alright?

Darren   Yeah. Nice place.

Lucy   Liar.

Darren   No, I'm not. Cosy int it?

Lucy   Could do with a clean. Messy cow me.

Darren   Me too.

Lucy   Messy bastard yer mean.

Darren   Yeah.

Lucy   Need a butler. Bloody Jeeves or somert. Wash me pots.

Darren   Should see me bedroom back 'ome.

Lucy   Dint think yer'd come.

Darren   'Course. Somert t'do, int it?

Lucy   Bit borin' like. Should o'brought some cards really. I'd o'got a couple o'board games if I'd known. Gran's got 'ole box o'games back 'ome. Guess 'oo. Buckaroo. Operation. Monopoly.

Darren   I like Cluedo me. Colonel Mustard.

Lucy   Colonel Custard.

Darren   All of 'em. Miss Scarlet.

Lucy   In the conservatory.

Darren   Wi'lead pipin' like, bosh.

Lucy   Do that again.

Darren   Eh?

Lucy   What yer did just then. Lead pipin'.

Darren   Oh. Bosh.

Lucy   You're funny you.

Pause.

Not too bored are yer?

Darren   I'm not bored.

Lucy   No, but once yer've lived 'ere a bit. Starin' at box all day.

She sits next to **Darren**.

Lucy   I like yer trainers. They new?

Darren   Yeah.

Lucy   Where d'yer get 'em?

Darren   Town.

Lucy   I like 'em. Adidas. I like the colour n'that.

Darren   D'yer?

Lucy   Yeah. They suit yer.

Darren   Love me trainers me.

Lucy   What size o'they?

Darren   Eh?

Lucy   Can I try 'em on?

Darren   What fu'?

Lucy   Somert t'do int it. What size o'they?

Darren   Eight.

Lucy   Gi'em us.

Darren   Too big f'you.

Lucy   No they're not, go on. Jus' forra sec like.

Darren *hesitates, then takes off his trainers.*

Lucy *takes them.*

Lucy   Must o'cost a bit.

Darren   Thirty quid. Knocked down from forty.

Lucy   Smart.

She puts on the trainers.

'Ey, they're alright these, aren't they?

She stands with the trainers.

Bouncy.

Lucy *walks round the flat, testing the trainers. Starts bouncing up and down on the spot.*

Darren   Gi'oer Lucy, yer'll wreck the soles.

Lucy   What Tiggers do best though int it? Can I keep 'em?

Darren   Eh? Yer jokin', aren't yer? I only bought 'em other day.

Lucy   Yeah, but they look better on me than they do you.

Darren   N'what am I gonna wear?

Lucy   Be an early Christmas present like.

Darren   No chance.

Lucy *sits next to* **Darren**.

Lucy   Suit me though, don't they? Don't they?

Pause.

Darren   Bit cold in 'ere int it?

Lucy   No one's forcin' yer to stay.

She moves to the heater and turns it on.

Said they were gonna fix us radiators. Bloody council. S'pposed to be doin' whole block like. Lazy bastards. You got radiators at your place?

Darren   Couple.

Lucy   I'm on a gas card me. Got a lekky key n'all.
Nightmare at Christmas.

Darren   Want some chips? Loaded wi'vinegar mind.
Love me vinegar me. Vinegar crackers.

Lucy   You eat funny don't yer?

Darren   Eh? No I don't.

Lucy   Funny like a camel. 'Ere, yer dint buy 'em from
Chinky did yer?

Darren   Down parade there?

Lucy   Yer did dint yer? Oh naow.

Darren   What?

Lucy   Shunt go there yer know?

Darren   Why not?

Lucy   'E wanks in batter.

Darren   'Oo?

Lucy   That Mr Fu. 'E wanks in batter.

Darren   No 'e dunt.

Lucy   Does.

Darren   No 'e dunt. Really?

Lucy   Yeah. Common knowledge that.

Darren   Since when?

Lucy   Since 'is car got robbed.

Darren   Eh?

Lucy   Dave told us. There were pubes in 'is fish cake.

Darren   Naow.

Lucy   That's 'ow they know, like. 'Ow else do they get there? 'E's a racist bastard that Mr Fu. Dunt like yer 'less yer fuckin' Chinky. Thinks we're all out t'rob 'im or somert. Bin there yonks n'all. Think 'e'd 'ave more sense.

Darren   Spunk?

Lucy   Yeah.

Darren   'E spunks up? Fuck that.

He wraps his chips up in the paper.

Fuck that. Uuurgh.

Lucy   I go by Blockbusters now.

Darren   Should get me stomach pumped.

Lucy   Burger King. Double whopper wi'cheese. Onion rings on giro day.

Darren   Could o'told me before.

Lucy   Thought yer knew.

Darren   Oh man!

He stands.

Quick, where's yer bog?

Lucy   Not gonna be sick, are yer?

Darren   No, jus' . . .

Darren *moves through the alcove, exits into the toilet.*

Lucy *spots a toothbrush poking out of* **Darren***'s jacket pocket. She takes it out, stands, moves to the alcove.*

Darren *re-enters.*

Lucy   Lookin' for this?

Darren (*awkwardly*)   Yeah. Cheers.

Darren *exits into the bathroom.*

Lucy *moves over to the cassette player, presses play. Music comes on, Bob Marley.* **Lucy** *exits into the kitchen.*

Darren *re-enters, holding the toothbrush. He sits and puts the toothbrush back in the jacket.*

Lucy *re-enters with two cans of lager.*

Lucy   You plannin' on stayin' the night?

Darren   Oh no, I . . .

Lucy *throws a can to* **Darren**, *who catches it.*

Darren   Tek it to work with us like.

Lucy   Yer can if yer like.

Pause.

Lucy *straightens her bed.* **Darren** *drinks from the can.*

Lucy   Sleep on floor n'that.

Pause.

Darren   You, er . . . Yer seein' anyone or anyone?

Lucy   What?

Darren   I 'eard about you n'Mr Lewis. Got sack in end dint 'e?

Lucy   Don't be so nosy. Nosy. Worse than them gets downstairs. Said yer could stop over, that's all.

Darren   Sorry. 'Ant seen yer, 'ave I?

Pause.

Lucy   Cheeky chops.

She sits by **Darren**.

Never change do yer? Remember at school yer were always flappin' 'bout somethin' someone told yer. Like Hislop when 'e said 'e 'ad cancer that time. Or when yer thought yer'd seen that ghost.

Darren   Naow.

Lucy   Yes yer did, I remember. In the physics lab.

Darren   Only forra week.

Lucy (*sings*)   Scaredy-cat, scaredy-cat, sittin' on the doormat.

Darren   Naow. It were just a shadow like. Weren't real.

Long pause.

Lucy   D'yer like Bob Marley?

Darren   'E's alright.

Lucy   Can't beat Bob, mate. Proper spiritual, aren't they? The songs. Could listen to 'im for hours. Like 'e's not dead, like 'e's bricked up in walls n'callin' out through plaster. Like Jesus.

Darren   Prefer R'n'B n'that. Destiny's Child. Brandy.

Lucy   I reckon 'e was Jesus. That's why 'e died so young.

Darren   Don't be stupid.

Lucy   Dave can't stand 'im. 'E's got shit taste in music, Dave. (*Pause.*) Me boyfriend like.

Darren   Oh.

Pause.

Lucy   You alright?

Darren   Yeah. Fine.

Lucy   'E's not like you. Dunt work like you.

Darren   Eh?

Lucy   Does me nut in. Treats me like dirt.

Darren   Oh. Should say somert.

Lucy   Yeah. I might n'all. Thanks.

Darren S'alright.

Lucy You're nice you.

Pause.

Yer got work tomorrow?

Darren Yeah. Wi'me uncle n'that.

Lucy Must be doin' well f'yersen now.

Darren Bin there ages now. Big job like. Gonna be great when it opens. Proper recordin' studio. F'the community, like. Massive n'all. 'Ad to totally rip place apart at first. Fuckin' rats everywhere.

Lucy Uuur.

Darren I know. Big fat things. Come up from chicken shop like. Tails like that. 'Ad to knock 'em on 'ead with me 'ammer.

Lucy Good money though. New pair o'trainers every week.

Darren Seen this? Tommy Hilfiger like.

Lucy That's good then, int it? Used to be a right scruffy sod at school.

Darren I know. Needed shootin'.

Lucy Yer gonna take the day off tomorrow?

Darren Jokin', aren't yer?

Lucy There's a pub round the corner. Don't ask for ID or owt. Go together cunt we?

Darren Me dad'd go mad, Luce. Sorry

Pause

Lucy Shit bein' seventeen int it? Never take us serious. Like bein' locked up.

Pause.

Lucy   Felt weird, dint it? Other day. Of all the bloody people.

Darren   I know. Good though.

Lucy   Just weird warnt it? All this time n'suddenly . . . 'Ere we are. Bosh.

Darren   Wi'lead pipin' n'that.

Lucy (*eagerly*)   Yeah. Dint think yer'd come.

Pause.

Could just say yer sick.

Darren   Delivery at ten.

Lucy   Never used t'stop yer before. 'Member they put you on one o'them report cards.

Darren   That were then though warnt it?

Lucy   That were then though warnt it?

Darren   Naow.

Lucy   Dint like school much did yer?

Darren   Were alright.

Lucy   Cunt stand it mesen. Never wagged it though. Not like you. What yer do? Used t'go off on yer own dint yer?

Darren   Not always.

Lucy   Wunt 'ave bottle, me.

Darren   Used to catch bus t'Barnsley like. Go the pictures. There were only ever me in there n'all. Could 'ave a fag n'everythin'.

Lucy   Honest?

Darren   'Member watchin' *Alien Resurrection* 'bout five times. Brilliant it wa'. Getting' into an eighteen n'that. There were this pub I used to go to. In Chapeltown. Sit n'ave a couple o'pints n'listen t'me Walkman.

Lucy   Alky.

Darren   I weren't no alky, that's just what everyone thought. I were only fourteen anyway. (*Pause.*) Don't ever think about it no more.

Lucy   Dint yer get bored?

Darren   Not really. Long as there were somert to watch. Better than school.

Lucy   Bit o'freedom, yeah?

Darren   Yeah.

Lucy   I like that.

Darren   Yeah?

Lucy   Yeah.

Darren   Fuckin' Barnsley though, int it?

Lucy   Yeah.

Pause.

Always thought yer fancied us.

Pause.

Weren't like all the others, were yer?

Pause.

Is it true what they said? When yer were sick that time? Why yer cunt do PE no more?

Pause.

Did it 'urt?

Pause.

Darren   'Ave t'go soon.

Pause.

What about you? You doin' owt?

Lucy Tomorrow?

Darren Yeah.

Lucy Sign on in the afternoon.

Darren Somert t'do, int it.

Lucy I got this guy. This Client Adviser. S'pposed t'be sendin' us up for all kinds, now I'm on New Deal n'that. Tried gettin' us some shitty typin' course one time, like fuck that. Secretary skills. I don't wanna be no secretary, not for no one. I told 'im n'all. Bloody lech. Must be about forty-odd. Swear. Can't keep 'is eyes off me tits.

Darren Oh. Right.

Lucy Keeps 'em off me back though.

Darren What time's last bus?

Lucy 'Bout five past.

Darren It's five past now.

Lucy Best get goin' then, 'ant yer?

Darren Gi'us me trainers.

Lucy Can't I keep 'em?

Darren No.

Pause.

Lucy 'E's not comin' back.

Darren Eh?

Lucy Dave. E's in Amsterdam at moment. 'Im n'is mate Gonzo. They saved up these coupons off *Sun*. Fuckin' thinks 'e's Denzel Washington or somert. Big bastard like that. Not like you.

Darren Oh.

Lucy Put a few pounds on 'ant yer?

Darren   Naow.

Lucy   Jelly belly.

Darren   Must be me mum's cookin' like.

Lucy   I like it though. Looks cute.

Darren   Karen 'ates it.

Lucy   Karen?

Darren   Yeah. Me girlfriend. Me girlfriend, Karen.

Lucy   Since when?

Darren   Few month back.

Lucy   Liar.

Darren   Lives down our road. Comes from Derby.
Loaded she is. Got 'er own car n'that. Ford Fiesta.

Lucy   Oh. Nice girl, yeah?

Darren   Yeah. Yeah, she is a bit.

Pause.

Lucy   Funny that. I thought you were a virgin still.

Darren   Eh?

Lucy   Yer look like a virgin.

Darren   Don't be stupid.

Lucy   She good in bed?

Darren   What?

Lucy   Karen. She good in bed?

Darren   Yeah, she's . . . She's fine.

Lucy   That's good then, int it? Remember at school.
Fretty. Best mates at one point, weren't yer?

Darren   Not really.

Lucy   Ren n'bloody Stimpy. Actin' up t'tatchers.

Darren   Only in first year.

Lucy   Said 'e taught you 'ow to wank.

Darren   Eh?

Lucy   Said yer used to camp out in 'is backyard and 'e told yer to imagine someone. Like yer'd never 'ad an 'ard-on before.

Darren   No I dint.

Lucy   'E said you imagined me.

Darren   You?

Lucy   But yer cunt cum or somert. Like it weren't developed enough.

Darren   Yer dint believe 'im, did yer?

Lucy   Yer ever wank over Karen? You 'ant, 'ave yer?

Darren   No.

Lucy   But yer did over me.

Darren   Course not.

Lucy   Yes yer did. I know yer did.

Pause.

Does she even know yer 'ere?

Darren   No, she's . . . She's at church.

Lucy   Never.

Darren   That's where I met 'er like.

Lucy   Oh my God. You never go fuckin' church.

Darren   Yeah. Course. Pentecostal like.

Lucy   All that gospel crap?

Darren   No it's not.

Lucy   Fuckin' crap.

Darren   Same as 'im.

Lucy: 'Oo?

Darren   Bob bloody Marley. Same as 'im.

Lucy   Gi'us a few verses then.

Darren   Eh?

Lucy   Sing us a song. Can just imagine you in one o'them white frocks.

Darren   It's nothin' like that. Oh, gi'oer.

Lucy   You've never shagged 'er 'ave yer?

Pause.

Darren   'Ant seen 'er all week.

Lucy   Not much of a girlfriend then is she?

Darren   Never said it were serious. (*Pause.*) Too posh.

Lucy   What?

Darren   Too posh.

Lucy   Like you, yer mean.

Darren   Naow.

Pause.

Lucy   Why d'yer come?

Darren   'Cause. We're friends, aren't we?

Lucy   Are we?

Darren   Course.

Lucy   What for ever?

Darren   Yeah.

Lucy   For ever and ever and ever?

Darren   I'm 'ere, aren't I?

Long pause.

Lucy   Still somert there, int they? Wunt've bumped into yer otherwise. There is though, int they?

Pause.

Got lovely brown eyes 'ant yer?

Pause.
Lucy *touches* **Darren**, *who clumsily responds.*
They kiss.
Pause.

Darren   They do suit yer, them.

Lucy   What?

Darren   Them trainers. They suit yer.

Lights fade.

Scene Two

A week later. Day.

Lucy, *in her dressing gown, holds the front door open.* **Dave** *is standing in the doorway, carrying a rucksack. Behind him is* **Gonzo**.

Dave   Fuck me, lass, yer deaf or what?

Lucy   You're lookin' well.

Dave   Mind out then.

Dave *and* **Gonzo** *let themselves in,* **Dave** *drops his rucksack by the door.*

Lucy   Caught the sun, 'ant yer?

Dave   Takin' the piss?

Lucy   You 'ave.

Gonzo   Move out, I'm bustin'.

Gonzo *whisks past* **Lucy** *and* **Dave** *and goes through into the bathroom.*

Dave   Yer missed us? 'Ere.

He digs in his jeans pocket and pulls out a small bag of skunk weed.

Bit of a present like. Donkey's knob.

Lucy   Eh?

Dave   That's what they call it. Donkey's knob. Superskunk. Thought yer'd appreciate it.

He hands **Lucy** *the weed.*

Proper potent n'all, so don't go mad.

Lucy   Were just about to run a bath.

Dave   What?

Lucy   Just now.

Dave   'Ant seen yer for over a week.

Lucy   Yeah and I've only just got me giro.

Dave   Aren't yer gonna gi'us a kiss?

He embraces and kisses **Lucy**. *The toilet flushes, offstage.*

Yer missed us? I've missed you.

Lucy   Yer know I 'ave.

Pause.

Dave *kisses* **Lucy**.

Lucy   There's a funfair just opened in Millhouses.

Dave   Oh. That's nice. So what?

Lucy   There's waltzers n'everythin'. D'yer have a nice time? Look like yer 'ave.

Dave   Fuckin' see why Anne Frank loved it so much.

Gonzo *re-enters from the toilet, wiping his hands on his jeans.*

Dave   Done a lot o'thinkin', 'ant we Gonz?

Gonzo   Eh?

Dave   Just tellin' Luce 'bout us plans. What we talked about.

Gonzo   Oh yeah.

Gonzo *sits on the bed and proceeds to build a spliff.*

Dave   I've missed yer, yer know? Med me realise. Not gettin' any younger are we?

Lucy   No. Eh? What d'yer mean younger?

Pause.
Dave *runs his fingers through* **Lucy***'s hair.*

Dave   Little bloody acorn you. 'Ere.

He moves **Lucy** *to the sofa, sits her down next to him.*

Skin one up f'yer if yer like.

He takes the bag of skunk off **Lucy***, proceeds to build a spliff.*

(*Crap Jamaican accent.*)   Bun-up a weed no-gal. T'roat jus' jingle wi'dat sweet-sweet madda 'erb t'rars.

He laughs at himself.

Fuckin' run out o'money, dint we? 'Ad t'blag it on train back to Rotterdam in end. On to ferry. Sneakin' through customs like a pair o'bloody schoolkids, weren't we, Gonz?

Gonzo   Jedi mind trick, star.

Dave: Yeah, fuckin' . . . Obi-Wan 'ere, gi'in it the old Crocodile Dundee wi'is fingers. 'Pretend we're invisible,' 'e sez. Through the barriers, half an ounce wedged under 'is bollocks, like, fuck me, 'ope yer 'ant got crabs or we'll all be fucked. Not that we . . . We dint get up to owt or nowt. Honest, Luce, yer should see 'em, down the red-light district n'that? Disgustin'. Big fat fuckin' . . . Russians mostly, I reckon. That or Japs. Fuckin' need a red light to cover up bruises. (*Pause.*) Sad really. We just stopped round coffee shops n'that. Bought mesen a T-shirt, look.

He rolls up his jumper and shows off his 'Bulldog Coffee Shop' T-shirt.

Good, innit? Just gettin' mashed like. Talkin'. Med a few promises, dint we, Gonz?

Gonzo   Yeah. Gonna be good boys from now on.

Dave   No more fuckin' shit. Strictly ganja. Start makin' an effort, innit? I mean, Gonzo's got a family to look after innit? 'Ow d'yer think they must feel? Kid never sees 'is dad no more.

Gonzo   Just get caught up in it all, don't yer? Routine of it.

Dave   I mean it, Luce. Look at me.

Lucy   What?

Dave   'Ave you even been listenin'?

Lucy   'Course.

Dave   Sat there like a cabbage.

Lucy   You 'ant said nowt.

Dave   F'fucksake . . .

Lucy   You 'ant. Barge in when I'm 'avin' a nice quiet day on me own, I'm a busy woman, Dave. Yer dint even send us a postcard.

Dave   I'm 'ere, aren't I?

Lucy   And what's 'e doin' 'ere? I told yer, I don't want 'im 'ere no more. Looks like a freak wi'that nose. Enough to give yer nightmares.

Dave (*laughs*)   Alright, alright . . .

Lucy   My flat, it's my flat, Dave.

Dave   Yeah, and 'e's a witness int 'e?

Lucy   Eh?

Dave   Stand up. Go on. Stand up.

Lucy   You stand up.

Dave   I'm tryin' to express mesen 'ere.

Lucy   Fine. Never listen to me anyway.

Dave   Look . . . 'Ow can I put this?

Gonzo   Bin doin' a lot o'thinkin'.

Dave   Bin doin' a lot o'thinkin'. 'Bout you n'me, Luce? That's 'alf reason we come back so soon.

Lucy   Thought that's why yer left in first place?

Dave   Yeah and I wanna mek it up to yer, don't I, Gonz?

Gonzo   Can't just run away.

Dave   That's a coward's way out. Honest, Luce, it's opened my eyes out there. Some right scabs. Junkies, fuckin' . . . 'Eadcases innit? I don't wanna end up like that, you don't wanna end up like that, lookin' like that. And I know it's been 'ard on both us, not just me. Fuckin' hate mesen the way I've . . . the way I've . . .

Gonzo   Taken 'er for granted.

Dave   In the past, like, in the past. Not, well . . . Yer know?

Lucy   Slept around.

Dave   Don't put it like that, that's not fair. Alright, it is fair, but that's what I'm sayin', Luce, it's over, I wanna . . . Wanna show yer that I can mek yer happy.

Lucy   I am 'appy.

Dave   No yer not.

Lucy   I am.

Dave   Lucy, you are not happy.

Lucy   But . . .

Dave   Lucy! (*Pause*) Only 'ave t'look at yer. Look at yer complexion f'fucksake. Too many takeaways that. Need to get a bit o'fruit down yer. Got the diet of a four-year-old, locked in 'ere all day wi'no one to look after yer. Cuts me up just thinkin' of it. Feel like a right fuckin' failure. 'Ere.

He stands and pulls **Lucy** *to her feet.*

Know what's comin', don't yer?

Lucy   Do I?

Dave   What we've always wanted these last six months. 'Ere, Gonz, get the camera, will yer?

Dave *gets down on one knee and digs into his pocket.* **Gonzo** *moves, goes to the rucksack and rummages inside.* **Dave** *pulls a ganja bag out of his pocket, inside is a cheap silver ring. He takes the ring out of the bag.*

Dave   'Ere.

He gives the ring to **Lucy**.

It's not real or owt. Thirty guilders. Stupid really. Always bin a bit of a softie, 'ant I?

Lucy   Since when?

Dave   Since I said, alright? – Don't bend it!

Lucy   I'm not.

Dave   Fucksake, Luce, just put it on, will yer? 'Ere.

Pause.

Dave *puts the ring on* **Lucy**'*s finger.*

I'm serious, yer know? I'll move in n'everythin'. Get Bill to get us a job on yard again.

Gonzo   Yer sure it's in 'ere?

Dave   Under me keks. Well? 'Ow about it? I will change. Promise. (*Pause.*) Can do it at the weekend if yer like. There's that registery office by the Novotel, yer pass it on bus. That is, if yer want to . . . Yer know? Start a family again.

Lucy   Again?

Dave *dithers, stands.*
Gonzo *finds the camera.*

Dave   Well, not . . . Obviously not again, but . . .

Lucy   Again.

Dave   No, I ...

Lucy   Like you n'Tanya, yer mean?

Dave   Don't be fuckin' stupid, o'course not, that were . . .

Lucy   Reason she left yer, weren't it?

Dave   Now listen . . .

Lucy   Fuckin' jaffa.

Dave   'Ey!

Lucy   Jaffa. Useless fuckin' . . .

Dave *strikes* **Lucy**.
Gonzo *takes a picture.*

Dave   Look, just ignore that, alright? (*Pause.*) Luce? Come on, yer know I dint mean it.

Lucy   Bastard.

Dave   Said I'm sorry, dint I?

He gets on his knee again.

(*To Lucy*)   Just slipped out like. Friends? (*Pause.*) Oh come on Luce, don't be a cunt all yer life.

He takes **Lucy**'s *hand.* **Lucy** *pulls away.*

Come on . . .

Lucy   Geddof me!

Gonzo *takes a picture.*

Dave   Gonzo!

Lucy   Two timin' waste o'space.

Lucy *pulls the off ring and throws it across the room.*

Dave   Lucy . . .

Lucy   Fuck off back t'yer barstool!

Lucy *exits into the bathroom.*
Pause.
Taps are heard running, offstage.
Dave *finds the ring.*

Dave (*to Gonzo*)   Don't you say nothin'.

Dave *moves to the bathroom door, knocks.*
Gonzo *sits and finishes building his spliff.*

Dave   'Ere, Luce. Be good though, wunt it? Be good though wunt it, Luce? Make a fresh start. Me dad won't know what's 'it 'im. Be like Madonna n'Guy Ritchie or somert. Posh n'Becks. Gonz as best man n'that. Show 'em what counts. Show 'em we can do it.

Lucy *re-enters.*

Lucy   You still 'ere?

Pause.
Lucy *searches for a towel among the piles of dirty clothes.*

Lucy   Old enough t'be me father, the state.

Dave   Someone been puttin' ideas into your 'ead? Lucy? They 'ave, 'ant they?

Lucy   Too much thinkin' does yer brain in anyway.

Dave   What?

Lucy *finds her towel.*

Lucy   Don't look at me like that. Crack'ead. Mongrel.
Dirty fuckin' . . .

Dave *kicks over the television. It smashes.*

Pause.

Lucy   So? That prove yerra man, does it?

Dave   No. No it dunt.

He gathers his belongings.

Pathetic.

Lucy   I know you are.

Dave   Women out there'd love to rip the pants off me, yer
know? Should count yer bloody chickens I stick wi'it. Lucky
I'm so patient. You want time t'think about it, fine, fuckin'
fine. But I'm not gonna be around for ever, Luce. I'm not
Dracula. Yer do realise that, don't yer?

Pause.

Well? Look at me, f'fucksake. I'm talkin', Luce.

Lucy   Yer'll pay f'that n'all. Yer will.

Pause.

Dave *tries to hug* **Lucy**, *who backs off.*

Lucy   Fuck off, will . . . ?!

Dave   Listen!

Lucy   No!

Dave   I forgive yer, alright? I forgive yer. (*Pause.*) 'Ere.

He digs in his pocket, pulls out a couple of notes – two fivers.

All I've got.

He gives **Lucy** *the notes.*

Treat yersen. On me, yeah? Get a pizza or somert.

Pause.
Lucy *stuffs the notes in her mouth, chews them up and spits them out.*
Dave *gathers the wet notes off the floor.*

Dave   Look . . . Look, just gi'us a call, yeah?

He takes his rucksack, moves to the door.

When yer ready.

Lucy   I've already told yer, Dave, I'm . . .

Dave   When yer ready, I said. Well?

Lucy *blows a raspberry.*

Dave   'Bout time you grew up, Luce.

Lucy   Would do if yer'd fuck off stalkin' me.

Dave   I will.

Lucy   Go on then.

Dave   I will.

Lucy   Run back to Daddy.

Dave   There's no turnin' back, yer know?

Lucy   Good.

Dave   This is it, Luce. Once I step out that door.

Lucy   Honest?

Dave   On the fuckin' cross, yeah.

Lucy   Can I 'ave that in writin'?

Dave   Yer gonna call us or what?

Lucy   Call you a cunt. Useless.

Dave   You are. Yer fuckin' are, Luce.

Lucy   Need a real man, me.

Dave   Oh yeah?

Lucy   Yeah. Someone 'oo dunt cream all over sheets before we've even started. True though, int it?

Dave   Bitch.

Lucy   That's me alright.

Dave   Yer'll see.

Lucy   Mel bloody B!

Dave   Don't know what's good f'yer!

Dave *exits, slamming the door.*
Pause.

Gonzo   Told 'im yer weren't worth it.

Lucy   You can get lost n'all. Bloody choke chain. Well, go on.

Gonzo *rests himself and lights his spliff.*
Lucy *goes to the television and puts it back in place.*
Long pause.
Darren, *in just his boxer shorts, crawls out from under the bed.*

Lucy   You alright? D'yer wanna cuppa?

Gonzo   'Ere, that's some bloody bedbug, Luce.

Lucy   See what I 'ave to put up with?

Gonzo   Should ring the council 'bout that.

Lucy   'Oo asked you?

Blackout.

Scene Three

A month later. Evening.

Lucy *and* **Nikki** *and* **Jo** *sit, drinking glasses of cheap wine, smoking. Plate of biscuits on the table. New second-hand television.*

Nikki   Can't believe it, can you?

Jo   No, God 'elp us.

Nikki   When d'yer find out?

Lucy   Last week.

Nikki   Arrr.

Pause.

Can't believe it.

Jo   Oh for . . . Would you cut it out?

Nikki   What?

Pause.
Lucy *nudges* **Nikki**.

Lucy   Can't believe it meself, Nik.

Nikki   Me neither. Thought of any names yet?

Lucy   Fucksake, Nikki, gi'us a chance.

Nikki   I like Fred me.

Lucy   Fred?

Nikki   What's wrong wi'Fred? It's different innit. Fred forra boy, Rose forra girl.

Jo *scowls at* **Nikki**.

Nikki   I'm jokin'.

Lucy   Might not call it owt. Just call it. (*Pulls a face.*)

Nikki   Eh?

Lucy   Well it's different innit.

Nikki   Won't get very far with a name like. (*Pulls a face.*) 'Ow's 'e gonna know when it's 'is teatime.

Lucy   Put it on table, won't I? 'E'll smell it.

Nikki   More like a dog than a kid.

Lucy   Tek after 'is dad then, won't 'e?

Pause.

Nikki   Mus' be made up.

Lucy   Yeah. Yeah I am.

Nikki   I think it's fab.

Jo   Jesus Christ.

Lucy   Oh, cheer up, Gran, it's not the end o'the world.

Jo   Yer said that last time.

Lucy   That were last time. Besides, I'm still 'ere, aren't I?

Jo   Just about.

Nikki   Oh, come on, it's not every day yer find out yer gonna be a great-grandmother.

Lucy   She'll come round.

Jo   S'ppose I'll 'ave to when yer run out o'bloody food.

Nikki   Oh, 'ave a biscuit n'shut up.

Lucy   Miserable old git.

Jo   'Ant you got a conscience? Thought yer'd've learnt yer lesson be now. Look. Look at it.

She signals to the framed picture of the toddler.

She's not dead, yer know?

Nikki   Gran!

Lucy   No, but she might as bloody well be.

Pause.

Nikki   Be alright t'come n'babysit, won't it?

Lucy   'Course. Once we're settled.

Nikki   I'm great wi'kids me.

Lucy   'Ope yer both hungry. Get an Indian in a bit. I'll send Darren on an errand.

Jo Oh, so 'e's got a name 'as 'e?

Lucy 'E's movin' in next week.

Nikki Arrr. Who's Darren?

Lucy Who d'yer think?

Nikki But . . . What 'appened t'Dave?

Lucy Kicked the telly over.

Nikki Oh. Oh! That's nice! Little portable, look.

Lucy Darren brought it over from 'is on New Year. Same night we conceived like.

Nikki Now how romantic is that.

Jo Please.

Nikki And t'think I was sat in wi'old misery guts 'ere.

Jo What d'yer mean? We 'ad a lovely night.

Nikki Yeah, right. Two words, Luce. Freddie bloody Mercury.

Lucy Oh, Gran.

Nikki Wish I'd never bought 'er that Queen video now. Never 'ear the end of it.

Jo Man's a legend.

Nikki I don't care.

Jo Man's a legend, Nikki.

Lucy Least yer dint 'ave the whole estate barkin' on till four in the mornin'. Drove me up the wall.

Nikki Can't stop people enjoyin' 'emselves, Luce.

Lucy It's not that I've got a problem with. It's all that Happy New Year's shite I can't stand. Fuckin' stupid. Me n'Darren sat in, right? All cosy on sofa there. Suddenly, stroke o'midnight, ding bloody dong. Fireworks on telly

n'that. Did me 'ead right in it did. All oer estate like.
Runnin' out o'flats like mice and on to balconies. All the
families givin' it whatsit. 'Old Land's Eye' n'that. Drownin'
out the flat like a bunch o'bloody moggies. N'I'm like, what?
Like we're all suddenly best mates or somert. I mean, every
other day o'the year, it's fuck you, don't wanna know yer.
Fuck you, out the way. But suddenly, turn o'century and it's
like, yeah, let's 'ave a bloody singalong. Pat each other on
the back and for what? So they can turn round next day and
stab yer in the back? Dunt mek sense. Even 'ad to stop
Darren joinin' in at one point.

Pause.

Nikki   Least yer conceived though, eh?

Lucy   We were dancin' all night.

Nikki   And the rest.

Lucy (*giggles*)   Yeah, well . . .

Nikki   Arrr, look at 'er, she's blushin', look.

Lucy   'E bought us flowers n'everythin'. Breakfast in bed.

Nikki   Arrr.

Lucy   He's got a job n'that. Renovations.

Nikki   I think it's dead sweet me. Wish Brendan was that
thoughtful.

Jo (*to Lucy*)   See what yer've done? Puttin' ideas in 'er 'ead.

Lucy   Takes two to tango, Gran. Learnt that off me mum.
Look at us two, f'fucksake. 'Ardly the bloody Brady Bunch,
are we?

Jo   That's not fair, Lucy.

Lucy   Well. Don't 'ear me complainin'.

Nikki   Lucky if I can drag 'im off that bloody PlayStation,
never mind no tango.

Lucy   Wunt stand for'it me.

Nikki   Should see 'is thumbs. Blisters all oer the ends there.

Lucy   Should chop 'em off.

Nikki   N'go out wi'some spastic? You're weird.

Lucy   Don't knock it. Know where yer stand wi' disabled. Know where their loyalties lie, for one. Long as yer make 'em feel human.

Nikki   What? And 'ave 'em wrigglin' under the covers 'cause they can't keep still?

Lucy   Why not?

Nikki   'Ave yer not seen 'em on the telly? Can't even talk right.

Lucy   Show us a bloke 'oo can.

Nikki   True. (*Pause.*) Cunt share same bed though still. Might start bitin' yer or somert. Dribblin' on yer shoulder – Uurgh.

Jo   Should 'ave you two lobotomised, talkin' like that. Disgustin'.

Nikki   Oh, 'ere she goes.

Jo   'Ant yer got no manners? They can't 'elp the way they look, poor sods.

Lucy   Never said they were poor.

Jo   Yer know what I mean, Lucy.

Lucy   Just statin' a fact. Yer know where you are wi'disabled. What's wrong wi'that? It's you who's turnin' 'em into some sort o'special case, Gran.

Nikki   Dunno if 'e even wants kids. Brendan, I mean. Never asked.

Lucy   What's to ask? Just gotta take a few days off, 'ant yer? 'E'll never know.

Nikki   What? Yer mean . . . ? No, I couldn't.

Jo   You leave 'er out o'this.

Lucy   She's gotta mind of 'er own.

Jo   Not with you around she 'ant.

Nikki   'Ey, d'yer mind?

Lucy   Pay no attention, Nik.

Nikki   Do what I want. My life.

Jo   Yes and if yer'd got any sense yer'd get yerself to college and learn somert before you end up like 'er.

Lucy   She's not an idiot, Gran.

Jo   Did you even look at that prospectus I got yer?

Nikki   Yeah.

Lucy   Give 'er a break, she's only just out o'school.

Jo   Only just. 'Ad to bend over backwards just to get 'er in the bloody exam 'all. And no, she's not an idiot. Four GCSE's she got in the end. Proud o'yer n'all, Nikki. F'Godsake, don't waste it.

Nikki   I'm not.

Lucy   Let 'er live a bit first, will yer?

Jo   That's what I'm tryin' to do, Lucy.

Lucy   By sendin' 'er to some poncey college wi'a bunch o'bloody lah-di-dah students.

Jo   There's countries'd kill for an education system like ours, Lucy. D'yer ever watch the news? There's kids your age in Africa don't even 'ave runnin' water never mind no . . .

Lucy   Let 'em fuckin' 'ave it then. Rather starve.

Jo Just a bloody game to you, isn't it?

Lucy I never learnt owt.

Jo Yer never even tried.

Lucy Yes I did, I were in top classes for ages.

Jo You were sleepin' with yer bloody form tutor!

Nikki Oh, come on, Gran, we've only just got 'ere.

Jo Yes and I'm sick t'the stomach already.

Nikki Give 'er a chance.

Jo No-good bloody . . .

She grabs her bag and coat.

Never learn, d'yer?

Lucy Must be genetic then innit?

Jo You need to learn some self-respect, girl. What d'yer think's gonna happen after that one drops?

Lucy Nothin'.

Jo Exactly. Nothin'. Wait till me or its dad or the bloody social come and tek it away, while yer . . . sit there and wait f'some other walkin' sperm bank come knockin' on the door. 'Ave you even 'ad a check-up?

Lucy What?

Jo AIDS, darlin', AIDS.

Lucy Cross that bridge when I come to it, won't I?

Nikki Lucy.

Lucy Don't you start n'all.

Nikki Gotta be careful now, yer know? Never know who . . .

Jo 'Course she's not bloody careful, look at 'er. Does 'e even know? This Dazwell.

Lucy   Darren.

Jo   Whatever. Yer sure it's even his?

Lucy   I'm not a slut, Gran.

Nikki   She's not.

Jo   Oh, shuddup, Nikki.

Nikki   Gran!

Lucy   Should be dead and buried be now anyway.

Nikki   'Ey! Don't say that.

Jo (*to* **Nikki**)   Come on. Get yer things together.

She pulls a Walkman out of her handbag and proceeds to put it on.

Can't believe I missed *Watchdog* f'this.

Jo, *with Walkman, exits through the alcove into the bathroom.*

Lucy   Should o'bloody poisoned yer!

Pause.

Nikki   Don't worry, she'll be alright in a minute. Life-saver that Walkman.

Pause.

Shunt o'said that, Luce. Yer know she's not bin well.

Lucy   Thought yer'd be pleased.

Nikki   'Course she's pleased, Luce, we both are. She's just old, yer know? Wunt even go n'cash 'er pension other day. 'Ad to do it for 'er while she sits at 'ome with 'er feet up. Like she's given up.

Pause.

Lucy   It is different. This time.

Nikki   Yer gonna get married?

Lucy   Dunno.

Nikki   Best thing in the world aren't they? Babies. Way the little faces scrunch up n'that. Don't know nothin' d'they? What they've got comin' to 'em n'that.

Lucy   I like their 'ands.

Pause.

Nikki   Wish yer'd come back 'ome.

Lucy   Eh?

Nikki   Wish yer'd . . .

Darren *enters through the front door.*

Lucy   Oh, 'ello!

Darren (*to Lucy*)   I need to talk t'yer.

Nikki   Is that 'im?

She gets up and hugs **Darren**.

Arrr, look at 'im. 'E's just a kid 'imself!

Lucy   I know.

Nikki   Like a tweenie.

Lucy   I know.

Nikki   It is Darren, yeah? 'Ey, congratulations . . .

Darren   Yeah . . .

Nikki   Lucy were just tellin' us.

Darren   Look, Luce . . .

Nikki   I'm Nikki, by the way.

Lucy   Don't be ignorant, Darren.

Darren   Pleased t'meet yer. Could I just . . .

Nikki   Lucy's told us all about yer.

Darren *moves past* **Nikki** *and goes to* **Lucy**.

Lucy   'Ad a good day?

Darren   Can we talk?

Lucy   'Course we can. Must be exhausted.

Nikki   'Ere, Gran! Darren's 'ere!

Darren   In private.

Lucy   This is private.

Nikki *knocks on the bathroom door.*

Nikki   Gran!

Darren   I need to . . .

Lucy   Don't I get a kiss on the cheek?

Nikki   'Urry up!

Darren   Look . . .

Lucy   Kiss please.

Darren *hesitates, then kisses* **Lucy** *on the cheek.*

Lucy   Thought we'd get an Indian in a bit.

Darren   Fucksake, listen to me, will yer?!

Nikki   Gran! What yer doin' in there?

Jo *enters from the bathroom, taking off her Walkman.*

Jo   What d'yer think I'm bloody – Oh, 'ello, duck.

Darren   Sorry, I dint mean to snap, it's just . . .

Nikki   Let's stay forra bit, eh? Come on.

Darren   Can we talk?

Jo   It's Darren, isn't it?

Nikki   That's our Gran.

Jo   I'm not a waxwork, Nikki. Name's Joan. Jo for short.

Darren *reluctantly shakes hands.*

Darren   Nice to meet yer.

Jo   Little sweetie, aren't yer?

Lucy   Don't be rude, Darren.

Jo   I hear yer in renovations.

Darren   Yeah. Family thing.

Lucy   Proper little businessman.

Jo   Really?

Nikki   Don't 'og 'im, Gran.

Jo   What yer doin' wi'this one then?

Nikki   Gran!

Jo   She payin' yer?

Darren   I'm not.

Jo   Sorry?

Darren   I'm not with anyone, alright? Lucy, please.

Lucy   Well, come on, sit down everyone, sit down.

Jo, **Nikki**, **Darren** and **Lucy** *sit down.*
Long pause.
Lucy *picks a selection of takeaway pamphlets.*

Lucy   Right. What would everyone like? They all deliver.
Golden Poppadum does a really nice korma, but it is a bit
dear. Could just 'ave a pizza, if yer like. Domino's do a
family meal, look. Chicken wings, garlic bread, bottle
o'Coke. Well? Darren?

Darren   I'm not 'ungry.

Lucy   Course you are. We're celebratin', aren't we? Well?

Pause.

Nikki   Lovely eyes.

Lucy   And teeth look.

Pause.

Jo   Yer sure this is 'im?

Nikki   Could just get some chips, cunt we? D'yer fancy chips, Luce?

Lucy   Was there somert yer wanted to tell me? Darren!

Darren: It's kind o'private, alright?

Lucy   Oh, don't worry 'bout these two. Lips are sealed, aren't they, girls?

Darren   This int a bloody joke, Luce.

Lucy   Who's jokin'?

Nikki   Look, maybe we should . . .

Lucy   Oh no yer don't.

Jo   Poor lad doesn't know what 'e's got 'imself in for.

Lucy   D'yer mind?

Jo   Yer not the first one either, son.

Lucy   'Ere, shall we make a toast, Nik?

Nikki   Eh?

Lucy   Raise yer glasses then. Come on. Come on.

*She raises her glass, as do **Nikki** and **Jo**, reluctantly.*

Don't be a gooseberry, Darren, join in.

Nikki   'E 'ant got nowt.

Lucy   Well 'e'll just 'ave to pretend, won't yer? Go on. (*Pause.*) Darren. Darren! Raise yer bloody glass! Now!

Darren *raises his hand, as though holding a glass.*

Lucy   The future.

Nikki/Jo (*dully*)   The future.

They drink.

Long pause.

Nikki So. Renovations, yeah?

Lucy Shall we just skip the main course? Don't move, alright?

Lucy *exits into the kitchen.*

Nikki Nice of yer to bring yer telly over.

Darren What?

Nikki The telly there. Really nice.

Darren Don't know what you're talkin' about, sorry.

Nikki Must be dead excited.

Jo It'll all end in tears, yer know?

Lucy *re-enters, with a cake on a plate and a carving knife. The cake is lopsided, stuffed with cream – a mess.*

Lucy 'Ere we are. Enough for everyone, look.

She sits, placing the cake down before them all.

Good, int it? Less personal when yer buy it from shop.

She cuts the cake into four quarters.

Don't mind eatin' with yer hands, do yer?

She hands the pieces out to **Nikki, Jo** *and* **Darren**.

Nikki Is that . . . ? It is n'all. Lucy.

Lucy What?

Nikki There's egg yolk in this. You 'ant mixed it right.

Lucy Yes I 'ave.

Jo Yer can't be serious, Lucy. Lucy.

Lucy Yer'll eat it won't yer, Darren?

Jo And die of bloody food poisoning.

Lucy   'Course yer will.

Nikki   Uuuuur.

Lucy   Come on, Darren.

Nikki   Yer smelt it?

Jo   Don't shove it in my face, Nikki, I'm . . .

Darren   Oh, f'fucksake!

Darren *throws his piece of cake down.*

Lucy   Darren!

Darren *moves to the front door, opens it.*

Lucy   Darren!

Darren (*to* **Jo** *and* **Nikki**)   Please. Could yer please just . . . ?

Lucy   Don't make a fuckin' fool o'me . . .

Darren   I don't know what she told . . .

Lucy   I'm warnin' yer, yer little . . .

Darren   Fuck you, alright? Fuck you, fuck yer cake, fuck yer whole fuckin' family, alright?!

Lucy *throws the pieces of cake at* **Darren**.
Pause.

Darren (*to* **Nikki** *and* **Jo**)   If yer don't mind.

Lucy *takes the last slice of cake and starts eating.*
Pause.
Jo *and* **Nikki** *gather their things together.*

Lucy   Yeah, that's right, take 'is side why not.

Nikki (*to* **Lucy**)   Yer gonna be alright? Give us a ring, yeah?

Pause.
Lucy *in a sulk, eating.*

Nikki   Luce?

Jo   Come on, love, come on.

Nikki *and* **Jo** *head towards the exit.* **Jo** *whispers in* **Darren** *'s ear.*
Nikki *and* **Jo** *exit.* **Darren** *shuts the door behind them.*
Long Pause.

Darren   Don't believe you.

Lucy   Yeah, well, someone's gotta make an effort, 'ant
they? Where were yer anyway? Said yer'd be 'ere by seven.

Darren   I'm sick o'this, Luce.

Lucy   Yeah and I'm sick o'waitin'.

Darren   Phone ringin' every 'alf-hour . . .

Lucy   What d'yer expect?

Darren   I thought I'd med meself clear. I'm not
interested. A man makes a mistake, alright? (*Pause.*) Just one
o'them things. (*Pause.*) An accident, f'fucksake, that's all it
were, a stupid accident. (*Pause.*) Long as we face up t'the
facts, show a bit o'maturity. I mean . . . (*Pause.*) Nob'dy's to
know, are they?

Pause.
*He digs into his pocket and pulls out a piece of paper with a phone
number on it.*

Look. 'Av got the number o'this clinic. 'Ere.

He hands the paper to **Lucy**.

Up Nether Edge? I'll pay for it. Use me savin's n'that.

Lucy *examines the paper.*

Darren   Go there in the mornin', if yer like. I'll tek the
day off 'specially.

Pause.

This int easy for me either, yer know?

Pause.

Tell yer what. (*Pause.*) I'll just go n'mek us both a drink, yeah? (*Pause.*) While yer think about it.

He exits into the kitchen.
Pause.
Lucy *puts the piece of paper down, stands.*

Darren (*off*)   Yer got any milk?

Lucy *takes the carving knife and moves to the kitchen.*

Darren (*off*)   Lucy?

Lucy *exits into the kitchen.*
Pause.

Darren (*off*)   Aaaahh! Fuckin' 'ell! Fuckin'! Aaaah!

Silence.
Pause.
Lucy *re-enters, goes to the chest of drawers, picks up the picture of the toddler. She sits. Stands the picture. She wipes her eyes and lights a fag.*
Darren *re-enters, his fingers are cut and badly bleeding.*

Darren   Fuckin' . . .

Darren *exits into the bathroom.*
Lucy *moves the TV, starts flicking through the channels.*
Darren *re-enters, wrapping toilet roll round his blood-sodden hand.*

Darren   Don't 'ave t'take this, yer know?

Lucy   Gotta learn some'ow.

Darren *sits on the bed, nurses his hand.*

Darren   What's wrong with yer?

Lucy   Nowt. What's wrong with you?

Pause.

Anyway. Not the first time yer've cut yerself, is it?

Long pause.

Lucy *stands, moves over to* **Darren**, *who is in agony. She sits by* **Darren**.

Darren   F'Chrissakes, Luce . . .

Lucy   Actin' all the big man.

Darren   It's just . . .

Lucy   Yer drippin' all over the lino. 'Ere.

Lucy *delicately takes* **Darren**'s *blood-sodden hand.*

Darren   Yer know I don't mean nothin' by it don't yer?

She slowly removes the toilet paper.

Lucy   Just get scared sometimes.

Lucy *slowly licks the wounds clean.*
Pause.

Lucy   There. That's better. Shall we start again?

Darren   I can't do it, Luce.

Lucy   Darren . . .

Darren   I can't.

Lucy   We're not murderers f'fucksake.

Darren   Well yer 'ant exactly med it easy for me, 'ave yer? (*Pause.*) Sorry.

Lucy   You walked out on me, remember?

Darren   I know.

Lucy   I know yer know.

Pause.

Darren   Shunt've even bin 'ere.

Pause. **Darren** *is torn for words.*

Lucy   So none of it meant nothin' no?

Darren   No. I mean, yes, 'course it did, yer know it did. It's just . . . It's just . . .

Lucy   What?

Darren   There's choices int there?

Lucy   Choices.

Darren   Choices.

Lucy   Right and wrong, yeah?

Darren   Don't do this t'me, Luce. Please.

Pause.

Lucy   D'yer believe in Hell?

Darren   Yeah. 'Course I bloody do.

Lucy   Scares the shit out o'me.

Pause.

Lucy   'Ere, see what me sister brought us

Lucy *finds Cleudo.*

Lucy   Still got all the pieces I think.

Lucy *sits with Cleudo.*
She opens the box.
Pause as she checks for the pieces.

Lucy   Takes yer back dunt it?

Darren   Too young f'this.

Lucy   Yer told yer dad yet?

Darren   Eh?

Lucy   'Bout us, yer told 'im 'bout us? Well?

Pause.

Lucy   Ooh, look. It's the dog from Monopoly, look. What's 'e doin' in there?

Darren I can't.

Lucy What?

Darren I can't. 'E'd go mad, Luce.

Darren *sits back on the bed, while* **Lucy** *looks through Cluedo.*
Darren *begins to cry.*

Lucy 'Ant seen yer in days, thought yer might . . . (*Stops.*)

Darren Yer don't know what 'e's like. If 'e knew . . .

Lucy It's Karen int it? Darren. She been puttin' ideas in your 'ead?

Darren No.

Lucy She 'as, 'ant she?

Darren It's nowt to do with 'er.

Lucy What is it then?

Darren All of 'em. If they knew, if they even knew I was 'ere . . .

Lucy Oh, baby. Don't cry. Don't cry.

Darren Jus' me dad . . .

Lucy *hugs* **Darren**.

Lucy Come on. (*Pause.*) Can't just stick it in the shit can we? What'll 'e think? (*Pause.*) I mean, yer do believe don't yer.

Darren Eh?

Lucy 'E died for our sins, Darren. 'E did.

Darren I know.

Lucy Tell yer what, I'll even come along if yer want. Church I mean. (*Pause.*) Proper little choir girl me, yer know? Could show that Karen a thing or two. (*Sings.*) 'Kum by yah, me lord, Kum by yah'. Should 'ear my Amazin' Grace. Bin known t'shatter milk floats that.

Darren *sniffles a laugh.*

Lucy   That's better.

Pause. **Lucy** *wipes* **Darren***'s face with her sleeve.*

Lucy   See? Dunt matter really.

She moves. She lights a candle by the bed and turns the light off. The only light in the room comes from the candle and the television.

That's better, int it? Sleep better now, can't we?

She kisses **Darren**.

Gonna be beautiful.

Darren   Yeah?

Lucy   Yeah.

She kisses **Darren**, *holding him tight.*
Pause.

Fuckin' beautiful.

Darren   Yeah.

Lucy   This is it now.

Darren   I know.

Lucy   Yer'll see.

She pulls **Darren***'s head on to her lap, stroking him.*
Pause.

All make sense in the end. You n'me. Our own little home.
Do it up a bit, like. Lick o'paint. Put a throw over that thing.
Frame on picture there. Love that picture. Sez somethin',
dunt it? Really somert special about that. Only ever notice it
when I'm . . . (*Pause.*) Be able to decorate won't we? Once
we're settled. Nice blue carpet. Blue or green at any rate,
long as it's furry. Able to walk barefoot then. Barefoot in us
dressin' gowns. Couple o'lamps. Bookshelf. Sofa. Coffee-
table. Spiderplant. Video. Hoover. Keep it all clean.
Washin' machine. Go Kwik Save on Sunday. Economize.

(*Pause.*) *Radio Times.* Jus' bein' 'ere. Together. You comin'
back from work, n'avin' a shower. Nice cold shower. Don't
even 'ave to say owt if yer don't want, dunt bother me.
Prefer it that way. Long as we both know. Long as it dunt
turn into owt. Jus' sittin' 'ere. Thinkin'. Lick o'paint on the
walls. Be lovely. (*Long pause.*) And Christmas. (*Long pause.*)
Stay in bed at weekends. Snuggled up like Teddy bears.
Won't even answer door. Nowt t'prove anymore. Long as
we both know. Long as we both know.

Lights fade.

Scene Four

Three months later. Morning.

*The flat is much the same, only messier. Two tins of yellow paint are
stacked by the wall, near the window. One of them is opened. By the
tins is a rollerbrush, smothered with dry crusty yellow paint, and a
dirty black palate. On the wall is a small patch of yellow paint, the
start of a failed job.*

Dave *and* **Gonzo** *sit together.* **Gonzo** *is preparing a crackpipe.*

Lucy *can be heard vomiting from the bathroom.*

Dave   Fuck me, 'av you 'eard it? Fuckin' Bride
o'Chewbacca in there. Bin like this f'days now.

Gonzo   She alright?

Dave   'Ant said owt.

Gonzo   Wunt worry about it, star. Our Jocy were same
when she were flyin' flag. Fuckin' pukin', shits, spinnin' out
like a fuckin' whizzed-up mongol. Distressin's not the word,
star. Whoooo! 'Ad to . . . yer know? Sort 'er out, like. Yer
know? Just t'save me bacon, like. Woman 'ad one o'them
whatsits? Kitchen utensil.

Dave   What, like a slotted spoon?

Gonzo   No, more like a whatsit skewer f'carvin' up yer joint like? Forked prongs n'shit, this close to me heart.

Dave   Fuck.

Gonzo   This close, star. I mean . . . Somert missin' there, int they?

Dave   Yeah.

Gonzo   Somert missin' there, like . . . Fuck off, yer know? Grown woman. Tellin' yer. Not easy bein' a man.

Dave   Not in this day n'age.

Gonzo   Not easy bein' a man.

Dave   That's what me dad said. Over the moon 'e is. Thought 'e were gonna pop 'is clogs when I told 'im.

Gonzo   Another one in fold.

Dave   Long bloody last.

Gonzo   All about bloodline though int it?

Dave   All we've got in end.

Gonzo   Mystery o'creation, star.

Dave   Big bang.

Gonzo   Somert like that.

Pause.
They laugh.

'Ere, pass us that pin there. Tight as me sister's fuckin' chaff this.

Dave *passes the pin to* **Gonzo**, *who prepares the crackpipe.*

Gonzo   Yep. Nowt like a baby t'send yer fuckin' west. Why d'yer think I'm such an insomniac? Like a bloody owl these days. Be growin' fuckin' feathers next.

Dave   Can't bloody wait, Gonz. Bin tryin' ages f'this.

Gonzo   You n'Luce like?

Dave   No me n'yer mum, Gonz, 'course me n'Luce.

Pause.

Thought I wa' . . . Yer know? Forra bit.

Gonzo   What, like . . . ?

Dave   Yeah. Don't tell no one though.

Gonzo   'Course.

Dave   'Ad a bust-up over it n'all. Well, you were there, weren't yer?

Gonzo   Reckon she wa' already gone?

Dave   Just before the 'oliday, like, yeah.

Gonzo   That explains it then. Fuckin' nervous system goes AWOL, dunt it? Fragile breed, star.

Dave: Get all 'et up over nowt. I mean, tek Luce there. Fuckin' needs an 'ug once in a while, yer know? Just t'soften 'er up. Very sensitive nature. Born t'be a mother like. I mean, she's already got one daughter. Fuckin' nob'ead teacher, right? English teacher when she were at school like. Raped 'er. Lost 'is job n'everythin'. 'Ad to move in 'ere. 'Im n'Luce like . . . Like Michael Douglas n'that. Sick. She were only fifteen at time.

Gonzo   Guy needs a slap.

Dave   That's where I come in, innit? Once 'e fucked off back to 'is wife. Lucy left on 'er tod wi'baby, I mean . . . Yer don't do that do yer?

Gonzo   'Ere.

Gonzo *passes* **Dave** *the crackpipe and the lighter.*

Dave   'Ad t'show 'im what's what.

Gonzo   Flattened 'im, yeah?

Dave   Smashed 'is windows dint I? Put a beer glass on 'is doorstep. 'Ad shit in it like.

Gonzo   Like it, star, like it.

Dave *lights and smokes the rock.* **Gonzo** *lights two cigarettes, smokes one, lets the other burn.*
Long pause.

Dave   Strange 'ow they bleed int it?

Gonzo   What's that?

Dave   Time 'o month n'that. Strange. Just think, all oer world, there's what? Billions upon billions o'women sat at 'ome right now, bleedin' the bloody knickers off. Lucky they don't live on the same street, innit? Be enough to flood the Thames that. 'Ave to get Moses back, sort it out sharpish.

Gonzo   Must be 'ard though.

Dave   Eh?

Gonzo   Must mek yer feel cursed or somert.

Dave   Oh, so that's why they're tryin' t'run the world. Period pains.

Lucy *enters from the bathroom in a long T-shirt. She looks awful. She goes to bed and tries to sleep.*

Long pause as **Dave** *and* **Gonzo** *smoke.*

Gonzo   *Big Breakfast*'ll be on soon.

Long pause.

Dave   Not the same wi'out Denise Van Outen.

Gonzo   Kelly Brook were good though.

Long pause.

Dave   Should put some music on.

Long pause.

Gonzo   What 'appened?

Dave   There's tapes in that box there.

Gonzo   No. T'the baby n'that.

Dave   Oh. Fuckin' social warnt it? Last year.

Long pause.
Gonzo *starts loading up another pipe.*

Gonzo   Start again though now, can't yer?

Dave   Due in November like. Couple o'months. Start movin' me stuff in.

Gonzo   Do it up a bit, yeah?

Dave   Don't remind me.

He signals out the paint pots.

Went schiz on me the other day. Only bought 'em to keep 'er 'appy and I told 'er, 'I'm not 'avin' you breathin' in a load o'fuckin' paint fumes.' Poor little thing'll be trippin' 'is nuts off wi'that lot on the walls. I mean, I will do it, but, yer know? Now's not the time is it? It's baby comes first. That's all that matters. Good clean birth, no messin'. (*Pause.*) Take 'em down park wi'football.

Gonzo   'Oo's that then?

Dave   Little un like. Bit o'togger. Swimmin' baths. I'm not 'avin' 'im bein' no fat fuck. Gotta fend f'yersen these days. Cruel fuckin' world out there.

Gonzo   Should take 'em boxin'.

Dave   Get a punchbag hooked up, yeah. Set o'gloves.

Gonzo   What if it's a girl?

Dave   Eh?

Gonzo   Never know

Dave (*pause*)   Long as she does 'er homework. Keeps off streets.

Pause.

Dave   Anyway.

He wrenches himself up and moves to the cassette recorder and the box of tapes. Starts looking through them.

F'fucksake, Luce.

Gonzo   What?

Dave   Bob Marley all the fuckin' time.

Gonzo   Need a bit o'bass line, star. 'Ant she got no 'ouse?

Dave   Lucky if I find a fuckin' kennel in this lot.

Gonzo *starts mixing the cigarette ash in the crack bowl.*

Dave   Simon n'Garfunkel.

Gonzo   'Oo?

Dave (*laughs*)   Simon n'Garfunkel, mate.

Gonzo (*laughs*)   Yer takin' the piss?

Dave   That's all she's got.

He puts on the tape, presses play. He moves back next to **Gonzo***, sits. 'Bridge over Troubled Water' comes on.* **Dave** *and* **Gonzo** *sit in silence for a few moments as the music plays. Then they burst out laughing.*

Dave   It's not mine!

Lucy *stirs.*

Lucy   Dave.

The laughing continues.

Dave.

The laughing continues.
She sits up in bed, crying.

Dave, please!

The laughing continues.

She rushes to the tape-recorder, switches it off, takes the tape out.

Yer know it makes me cry, it always makes me cry.

The laughing continues.
Lucy *goes back to bed.*
The laughter subsides.

Dave   Fucksake, Luce, we were listenin' t'that!

Pause.

Luce! . . . Lucy! 'Ey!

Dave *gets up, moves over to the bed.*
Gonzo *continues mixing the ash with the rock, subsequently smoking it as the dialogue continues.*

Dave   Lucy.

*He shakes **Lucy**.*

'Ey.

Lucy (*from under the covers*)   What yer 'ave t'do that for? Yer know what it does t'me.

Dave   Oh, come on, Luce, it's only a song. 'Ere.

*He sits on the bed and lifts **Lucy** up, who is clutching the cassette, tears in her eyes.*

(*Laughs.*)   Need a bloody crane f'yer soon, won't we? Come on now.

He takes the cassette from her.

Lucy   Can't sleep.

Dave   What?

Lucy   Can't sleep wi'your. Noisy bastards.

Dave   Don't be like that.

Dave *stands, lifts **Lucy** off the bed.*

Lucy   Dave.

Dave   Come on. I wanna show Gonz.

Lucy   I'm tired.

Dave   Thought yer cunt sleep.

Lucy   I can't.

Dave   Well then.

He escorts **Lucy** *and seats her between him and* **Gonzo**. **Gonzo** *smoking the pipe.*

See? Better already.

Lucy *grabs an Argos catalogue.*

Lucy   S'pposed t'be goin' shoppin' today.

Dave   Yeah. Gonzo's gonna drive us, aren't yer?

Gonzo   What?

Lucy   'Elp me decide then.

Dave   I am.

Lucy   S'pposed to be a family now.

Dave   We are, Luce. Why d'yer think I – 'Ere save a bit f'me, yer fuck.

Gonzo   Only jus' sparked it.

Dave   Fuck off, will yer?

Gonzo   Yeah, n'there's still . . .

Dave   Put it down.

Gonzo   . . . two bits there . . .

Dave   Gonzo.

Gonzo   It's fuckin' dust, look.

Dave   'Ey!

Gonzo (*puts pipe down*)   Dust.

Dave   I know what yer like, mate.

He grabs the pipe and the lighter, sparks up the pipe. **Lucy** *is flicking through the Argos catalogue.*

Dave   Oh look, there's fuck all there.

Gonzo   I told yer it's dust.

Dave   Where? I don't see no dust. Just fuckin' foil, look. Dead.

Gonzo   Alright, I'll load one up then.

Dave   Cheap scammin' twat.

Gonzo   Fucksake, Dave.

Dave   You 'ant 'idden none, 'ave yer? There were three there a minute ago.

Gonzo   What d'yer think that was?

Dave   What?

Gonzo   Just then. Before.

Dave   There were three there, Gonz.

Gonzo   Yeah, three includin' the one we just . . .

Dave   Bollocks, mate. One, two, three. There were three.

Gonzo *starts loading up the pipe.* **Dave** *starts searching round the floor.*

Dave   Fuck this. I know what I saw.

Gonzo   Wastin' yer time, star.

Dave   Fuckin' . . . I saw it, mate. Just . . .

Pause as he searches.

. . . two seconds ago.

Gonzo (*laughs*)   Dave, mate, there int nothin' there.

Dave *gets up off the floor.*

Dave   Yer dint pick it up, did yer?

Gonzo   Eh?

Dave *leans over* **Lucy** *and rummages through* **Gonzo**'s *shirt pocket.*

Gonzo   Dave!

Dave   Yer did, dint yer? Probably shoved it up yer big fuckin' beak there, innit? Come on . . .

Gonzo   What?

Dave   On yer feet, come on.

Gonzo   F'fucksake, 'ere!

He stands, pulls a rock, wrapped in a Rizla, from his jeans pocket.

'Appy now?

Gonzo *sits and gives the rock to* **Dave**.
Dave *unwraps the rock, checks it.*

Dave   Fuckin' slippery little cunt, you, aren't yer? Go on then, rack it up.

Gonzo   Yeah, well, if yer'd stop fuckin' frettin' forra minute.

Pause.
He starts loading up the pipe.

Last time though, yeah?

Dave   'Course. First proper binge in ages this.

Gonzo   Guess it dunt 'urt once in a while, does it?

Dave   Yeah. Dunt 'urt no one.

Pause.

Sorry 'bout that.

Gonzo   Don't be fuckin' . . .

Dave   No, yer know? Just get stupid innit?

Pause.

Gonzo   Want another? 'Ere.

Gonzo *digs in his pocket, pulls out a rock.*

Dave   On tik like? Fuckin' skint.

Gonzo   Whenever, star, whenever.

Gonzo *lights and smokes the pipe.*

Dave   Be fuckin' good wunt it? Go on 'oliday again like.
Sail out t'Dam. Me n'you. Be great wunt it, Gonz? (*Pause.*) .

Gonzo *passes the pipe to* **Dave**.
Dave *smokes.*
Long pause.

Dave (*to Lucy*)   You alright? See owt yer like?

Lucy   Quilt covers.

Dave   Yeah?

Lucy   Look.

Dave *looks at the catalogue.*

Dave   Got everythin' at Argos, 'ant they?

Lucy   Yeah.

Dave   Just gotta tap in the numbers.

Lucy   Yeah.

Dave *winks at* **Gonzo**.

Dave   Go there later then can't we?

Lucy *holds* **Dave**'s *hand, flicking through the catalogue.*
Pause.

Dave   'Ere, Gonz. Gonzo.

Gonzo   What?

Dave   Looks good, dunt she?

Gonzo   S'ppose.

Dave *feels* **Lucy***'s belly.*

Dave   Can feel it movin' sometimes. 'Ere.

He takes the catalogue off **Lucy***.*

Go on. Touch it.

Gonzo   Eh?

Lucy   Dave!

Dave   Go on.

Gonzo   What? Yer sure, like?

Lucy   'Ant finished yet.

Dave   Gonzo.

Pause.

Gonzo *puts his hand on* **Lucy***'s belly.*

Gonzo   Alright that, int it?

Dave   Can yer feel owt?

Gonzo   Not really.

Dave   Notice the way 'er lips've come up. All full like.

Gonzo   Oh yeah.

Dave   And 'er skin's cleared up.

Gonzo   Fuck.

Dave   Run yer fingers through 'er 'air. Like this. Won't bite or nothin'.

Gonzo *does as he is told.*

Dave   'Ant washed it all week either. What d'yer think?

Gonzo   Nice. Very clean.

Lucy   We're s'pposed t'be a family.

Dave   We are.

Lucy   Dunt feel like it. Dunt feel like owt no more. Sat on yer big fat arse. Get a job 'e sez.

Dave   I'm tryin'.

Lucy   In yer dreams.

Dave   There int nothin' goin', Luce.

Lucy   'Ant even looked.

Dave   Yer don't know what it's like out there. Grown man like me, can't even get a job stacking shelves. It's humiliatin', Luce. Talked down to by kids 'alf my age.

Lucy   I'm 'alf your age.

Dave   What?

Lucy   That 'ow yer feel about me, is it? Humiliated? Shamed to even tek me out the 'ouse case someone sees.

Dave   No.

Lucy   'Cause that's 'ow it fuckin' feels.

Dave   Oh, come on, Luce, yer just bein' stupid now.

Lucy   Yeah, well, 'ow's it gonna be when we 'ave guests round eh? What they gonna think with shit all over the floor? No fuckin' money, no nothin'. Pinocchio there, sat like a ferret. It's not normal, Dave.

Dave   Lucy.

Lucy   I 'ate it. Fuckin' chose this colour and it just sits there growin' skin.

Dave   Yer not even rollin' it right. It's up n'down, Luce, not sideways. Up n'down. F'fucksake, give it 'ere . . .

He grabs **Lucy**'s *painting arm. She refuses to stop.*

Be'ave, will yer?! Lucy!

Lucy *turns, smearing* **Dave**'s *face with the rollerbrush.*

Dave   Jesus . . .

Lucy *giggles, there is a slight struggle,* **Dave** *knocks the roller out of her hand.*

Dave   Fuckin' . . .

Lucy, *giggling, backs away, holding the tin of paint.* **Dave** *wipes the paint out of his eyes.*

Dave   Little . . . !

He approaches **Lucy**, *who starts flicking paint at him.*

'Ey!

Lucy, *giggling, backs across the room, flicking paint at* **Dave**, *who moves after her.* **Gonzo** *jumpily avoids the paint, protecting the crackpipe.*

Dave   One more, fuckin' . . . I'm warnin' yer, Luce . . . Gimme the . . .

Dave *grabs* **Lucy** *by the hair.*

Lucy   Ow!!

Dave *pulls the can of paint out of* **Lucy**'s *hand.*

Dave   D'yer know 'ow much that cost me?!

Dave *lets go of* **Lucy**, *marches across the room and puts the tin of paint back by the wall.*

Lucy   You're no fun, you.

Dave   Should fuckin' certify yer! Brand new shirt.

He exits into the bathroom, slamming the door.
Pause.

Dave (*off*)   Christ!

Gonzo *prepares his crackpipe.*
Pause.

Gonzo   Want some o'this? (*Pause.*) There's enough, like.

Lucy   Eh?

Gonzo   'Ello. Earth callin' Lucy.

Lucy   What?

Gonzo   Want some o'this? 'Ave t'be quick about it mind.
'Ere.

Lucy *sits.*
Gonzo *passes the pipe and the lighter to* **Lucy***.*

Gonzo   Just tek it slow, yeah? Let it linger in yer mouth.
Like a cigar or somert. (*Pause.*) Well, go on then.

Lucy *lights the rock and takes her first pull.*

Gonzo   Slowly. That's it.

Pause.
Lucy *takes another pull.*

Gonzo   Alright, alright, int bloody Olympics.

Gonzo *takes the pipe. He quickly adds cigarette ash to the bowl.*
Pause.
Lucy *sits back. Ever so slowly she exhales the smoke.*
Long pause.

Gonzo   Nowt tastes like this shit. Lingers in yer gob like
. . . Like palm o'violets or somert. (*Pause.*) Good, yeah?
Never forget that either.

He digs in his pocket and pulls out a scrap of paper.

Keep it under yer 'at though, yeah?

Lucy *takes the paper. She strokes* **Gonzo***'s nose. He grabs her hand.*

Gonzo   'Ey. What 'ave I said about that.

Lucy   Worried what 'e'll say?

Pause.

Think you own this place, don't yer?

The bathroom door opens. **Gonzo** *grabs the scrap of paper out of* **Lucy***'s hand and stuffs it in his pocket.*

Dave *enters. He moves to the bed and sits.*

Dave   'Ey. (*Pause.*) Lucy. Lucy.

Lucy   What?

Dave   Come 'ere.

Pause.

It'll get done, alright? Promise.

Lucy   Said that last time.

Dave   I mean it. I'll gi'Bill a ring. Must be somert goin'. Sweep up the fuckin' sawdust if I 'ave to. Promise.

Pause.
Lucy *wrenches herself up and moves to* **Dave***. She sits on the bed.* **Gonzo** *carries on regardless. Pause.*

Lucy   Strip off then.

Dave   Eh?

Lucy   'Cause. Just cuddle n'that.

Dave   But . . .

Lucy   Won't say owt will yer, Gonz? (*Pause.*) See? Go on.

Dave *laughs.* **Lucy** *laughs with him.*

Lucy   Go on.

Dave   Not on me own I'm not.

Lucy   Wanna see.

Dave   Gi'oer.

Lucy   Wanna see now. Please.

Pause.

Dave   Gi'us a blow job, like.

Lucy   No.

Dave   I'll gi'you one.

Lucy   No, Dave.

Dave   Dunt make sense otherwise.

Lucy   Give 'im one if yer don't.

Dave   What?

Lucy   I will won't I, Gonz? Probably bigger than yours anyway.

Long pause. **Dave** *and* **Lucy** *laugh/giggle.*

Dave   Come 'ere you.

Dave *holds* **Lucy**.

Lucy   Can 'ear 'im, Dave.

Dave   Mm?

Lucy   Listen. Can 'ear 'im.

Long pause.

Dave   Sometimes feel like cryin'. Yer know?

Pause.

Lights fade.

Scene Five

Five months later. Night.

The flat is decorated with balloons, streamers, and a banner pinned up on the backwall, which reads 'CONGRATULATIONS!'

Lucy *and* **Jo** *sit on the floor, playing Cluedo.* **Lucy** *wears a nightie and has a hospital band strapped to her wrist. Her feet and ankles are stained with mud and dirt.* **Lucy** *pulls the cards out of the little black envelope.*

Lucy   Ah, see that's where yer wrong. It were the spanner not the rope.

Jo   Oh well. Never mind, eh?

Lucy   Must be a card missin'.

Jo   Yes.

Lucy   Shall we 'ave another?

Jo   I don't think we've got time, dear.

Lucy   Course we 'ave! All the time in the world, come on.

Jo *takes her mobile phone out of her handbag.*

Lucy   Come on, Gran.

Jo *dials a number, waits for an answer.*
Lucy *sets up the pieces for another game of 'Cluedo'.*

Lucy   Just upset yer lost, aren't yer? It's only a game.

Jo   'Ello, Nikki? . . . Where? . . . Well, 'urry up about it will yer? . . . Yes. . . . Yes, I know it's . . . Tell 'im to put 'is foot down then.

Jo *turns the phone off.*

Lucy   Cheer up.

Jo   Why d'yer do it, eh? Lucy?

Lucy   You playin' or what?

Jo   Like that.

Lucy   What?

Jo   Dressed like that. In the middle o'the bloody night?

Lucy   Took a short cut through woods.

Jo   Been worried sick.

Lucy   I was bored.

Jo   It's got to stop, Lucy.

Lucy   It's got to stop, Lucy.

Jo   There's a baby back there needs its mother.

Lucy   Gi'it one then.

Jo   What?

Lucy   A mother, gi'it a mother.

Jo   Should wring your bloody neck.

Lucy   Like an ostrich. Neck like an ostrich.

Jo   I give up.

Lucy   That's what the teachers used t'say.

Jo   Yeah, there were some said a lot o'bloody things.

Lucy   Taught me more than you ever did. Don't stare.
Don't stare, I said. Worse than them bloody Shipmans, treat
me like a geriatric. Can fuckin' stuff their needles. Stuff 'em
up their arse. Try n'take me away, well? Sit down if yer
stayin'.

Jo   Yer sister'll be 'ere in a minute.

Lucy   I'm not movin'.

Jo   You haven't got a choice, Luce. You can't just . . .

Lucy   Fuckin' make it then!

Jo   Eh?

Lucy   A game, let's play another game, Gran.

Jo   If 'e comes, if 'e finds yer 'ere . . .

Lucy   Borin'.

Jo   Took five of 'em to hold 'im down back there. You
heard him, Lucy.

Lucy   'E'll come round.

Jo   Not now 'e won't.

Lucy   Always do. Yer don't know 'im, Gran, what 'e's like. I writ 'im a letter n'everythin'. On the side there.

Jo *finds the letter. She scans through it.*

Lucy   Weren't my fault. Weren't anyone's fault really. I mean, every couple 'as its ups n'downs.

Jo   Pack o'bloody lies.

Lucy   Be back on our feet in no time.

Jo   Should be ashamed of yerself.

Lucy   In no time. Yer'll see. More to life than this. What yer feel that counts. What's between us. What none o'you ever fuckin' see.

Pause.

If Darren was 'ere he'd play. Break 'is arm for me.

Jo   Oh darlin'.

She embraces **Lucy**, *kisses her.*

What happened, eh?

Lucy   Giv'oer, Gran! I'm not a kid.

Pause.

What?

Pause.

Jo   Come on. Let's get you dressed, eh?

She moves to the chest of drawers and removes items of clothing.

Surprised yer never freezed to death.

Lucy   Wish you'd make up yer mind. Thought we were gonna play.

Jo   Once we get 'ome.

Lucy   I am 'ome.

Pause.

Jo   She is a beautiful little thing.

Lucy *shrugs.*

Jo   Just need t'spend some time together, that's all.

Lucy   'Er 'ead throbs.

Jo   What?

Lucy   Dint wanna girl anyway.

Jo   Oh, come on . . .

Lucy   Not what we need though, is it? Another fuckin'
cunt in the family.

Jo   'Ey!

Lucy   Well . . .

Jo   Don't you ever speak about our . . .

Lucy   It's true.

Jo   . . . family like that again, you 'ear?! (*Pause.*) After all
we've been through, Lucy, f'Chrissakes.

Pause.
Jo *takes* **Lucy***'s socks, tries fitting them on* **Lucy***'s feet.* **Lucy**
struggles, laughing.

Lucy (*giggling*)   What yer doin'? Gran!

Jo   I've already told you, dear, yer sister's going to be . . .

Lucy   Gran! Stop it, will yer?!

Jo   You bloody do it then.

Lucy   Yer ticklin' me!

Jo *moves away, as* **Lucy** *laughs.* **Jo** *tries ringing Nikki again.*
Pause.

Lucy   Don't stop.

Pause.

Wish we'd played like this before. Gran? Gran.

Jo (*to the phone*)   Come on, come on . . .

Lucy *starts sorting the Cluedo cards into piles.*

Lucy   Be mad if they were real, wunt it? Real people, I mean. Looks like you that Mrs White.

Jo *turns the phone off.*
Pause.
Jo *sits on the bed, watching* **Lucy***, who sorts through the cards.*
Pause.

Jo   Can see why they fall at yer feet.

Lucy (*absently*)   Eh?

Jo   Take after yer mother.

Pause.

Hm. I weren't no cream tea either.

Lucy   It's Nikki I worry about.

Jo   I know how yer feel, Lucy. Really I do.

Lucy   What d'yer want, a medal?

Longer pause.

Jo   Could o'done more couldn't I? Yer can say it. I know. (*Pause.*) We all miss 'er, Lucy. (*Pause.*) Goin' to make it up t'yer n'all. Yer'll see. (*Pause.*) Just . . . Just tell me what . . .

Lucy   There. I've done it, look. It's the ballroom that's gone. (*Pause.*) You alright? (*Pause.*) Stupid game anyway. Everyone's got computers now, 'ant they?

Jo   Is that what yer'd like?

Lucy   Eh?

Jo   Brendan's got a computer.

Lucy   Who?

Jo   Nikki's boyfriend. Ask 'im nicely 'e might lend you it.

Lucy   Is 'e handsome?

Jo   Depends.

Lucy   Depends what yer mean by handsome?

Jo   Not really.

Lucy   Oh. She does love 'im though, dunt she?

Jo   There'll be 'ere soon anyway. Yer should ask her.

Lucy   She'll just laugh. I like the way she laughs.

Pause.

Dave's handsome int 'e? It's the skin. Constant. Like varnish. Wunt be seen dead wi'no ugly bloke. Not outside anyway. Not wi'everyone pointin'. All pink n'blemished n'all the wrong clothes.

Jo   Sound like yer grandad.

Lucy   Shall we play hide n'seek? Be good that. Before 'e gets back. You hide, and I'll count to sixty.

Jo   He's not coming back, Lucy.

Lucy   What?

Jo   He's not coming anywhere.

Lucy   'Course he is. Always does.

Jo   Not any more.

Lucy   Gettin' married in the spring. We are. We are. I thought yer knew.

Jo   Help yer buy a dress if yer want.

Lucy   Would yer?

Jo   Go town together. That shop by Debenhams.

Lucy   Big white thing in the window?

Jo   Yes.

Lucy   With a veil?

Jo   With a veil.

Lucy   Oh.

Jo   Can't go dressed like that.

Lucy   Yer can be a bridesmaid if yer want.

Jo   Well . . .

Lucy   Make my day that.

Jo   I'm a bit old to be a bridesmaid, dear.

Lucy   No yer not. No such thing as age. Long as yer wear contact lenses.

Jo   It's your day.

Lucy   You got married, dint yer?

Jo   Wasn't much choice with my parents.

Lucy   I know what yer mean. (*Pause.*) Remember 'e used to 'ave tongue in 'is sandwiches. (*Pause.*) Did yer ever go on honeymoon?

Jo   Blackpool.

Lucy   Pleasure beach n'that. We're gonna go Jamaica.

Jo   Lovely.

Lucy   On the beach. Where Bob grew up.

Jo   Get a nice tan.

Lucy   Yeah. That or Spain. Dunt make sense stayin' 'ere. All the same in this country. Never feel like yer've gone nowhere. Too many people. Too small.

Jo   You're cold, aren't you? I am.

Lucy   No gas.

Jo   Freezin'.

Lucy   Really? Should light some candles.

Jo   Put some clothes on more like.

Lucy   Yer gonna stay? You never stay, not once.

Jo   I am now.

Lucy   Would yer?

Jo   'Ere.

She takes the clothes off the bed and moves to **Lucy**.

Make yer look beautiful. Come on.

She lifts **Lucy** *up.*

Lucy   Need some make-up.

Jo   One thing at a time.

She dresses **Lucy**.
Pause.

Look at yer. Should never 'ave let yer go in first place.

Lucy   Could bottle me up n'sell us as perfume, cunt yer?
Or pop. Fizzy pop.

Jo   I'm not gonna watch same 'appen t'you, Lucy, I'm not.
You 'ear me? Not again.

Lucy   Wunt be enough to go round though, would there
really?

Jo   Likes o'that idiot, treatin' yer like a . . . Like that, like
meat and for what?

Lucy   'E will come back, won't 'e, Gran?

Jo   Could be so bloody simple.

Lucy   Won't be the same otherwise.

Jo   I dunno. Someone should bomb this bloody country.
That'd wake us up a bit. Saddam Hussein or someone. IRA,
bleedin' whatsisface? Bin Laden. Yeah. He could do it.
Drop a few tons of anthrax. Teach us what it really means
to suffer.

Lucy   D'yer wanna pick me? Pick me spots. Got tons
o'black'eads, me. Deep down. Be like monkeys, won't we?

Jo *strokes* **Lucy***'s face.*

Jo   Hm. Sweet.

Pause.

Lucy   I like that.

Pause.

Dave *enters through the front door, with a bag.*
Pause.

Lucy   See? Told yer dint I?

Jo   You stay away from 'er, 'ear?

Dave *ignores* **Jo** *and starts moving round the room, collecting his
belongings (mainly clothes) and stuffing them in the bag.*

Lucy   Dave?

Jo   Come on.

Lucy   Dave, what's wrong?

Jo   Put yer jacket on.

Lucy   I writ yer a letter, Dave, look.

Jo   Come on. Put it on, Lucy.

Jo *tries draping the jacket on* **Lucy**, **Lucy** *pushes her away.*

Lucy   Geddof me! Dave . . .

She tries approaching **Dave**, *who carries on regardless.*

Dave, please, talk to me. Talk to me, Dave.

Pause.

Just bein' silly now.

Jo Leave it.

Pause.

Lucy D'yer want some ice cream? Dave? It's yer favourite.

Lucy *exits into the kitchen.*
Pause.
Dave *finishes packing his bag.*

Jo Yer thought what yer gonna do?

Lucy *re-enters with a bowl of ice cream and a spoon.*

Lucy 'Ere we are. Great big oofus.

Dave *takes the bowl of ice cream. Doesn't move.*
Pause.

Dave Does 'e know?

Lucy What?

Dave Does 'e know?

Lucy What yer talkin' 'bout? Sit down. Sit down, Dave. 'Ant seen yer in days. Look at the balloons look.

Pause.
Jo *takes the bowl of ice cream off* **Dave**, *escorts him to the door.*

Lucy Gran! 'E 'ant even started yet. Tell 'er, Dave. 'E 'ant even started. 'E 'ant even started.

Dave *exits.*

Lucy Dave! Dave, wait!

She grabs her letter, exits, running after **Dave**.

Lucy (*off*) Dave!

Pause.

Jo *sits on the bed. The mobile phone rings. She sighs, and takes her glasses off. The mobile phone stops ringing.*
Lucy *re-enters, slamming the door, holding the letter.*

Jo   Can 'ardly blame 'im for being upset, Lucy.

Lucy   You told 'im, dint yer?

Jo   Told 'im?

Lucy   Were you.

Jo   Told 'im what?

Lucy   All along.

Jo   It were bloody obvious, Luce.

Lucy   Should o'known.

Jo   Only 'ad to look at 'er!

Lucy   Old fuckin' four-eyed cunt!

Jo   Only had to look at 'er, Lucy. What's wrong with yer? You expect him to just change overnight? It's not my fault, Lucy, you knew.

Lucy   Liar.

Jo   You knew what was going to –

Lucy   Yer always lyin'.

Jo   Look, say what yer like, Lucy, you just say what –

Lucy   I will.

Jo   Yer livin' in a dream world!

Lucy   Done it now. Done it now, 'ant yer?

Jo   F'Chrissakes –

Lucy   Useless fuckin' –

Jo   Don't blame me f'your fuckin' –

Lucy   That why yer told 'im? Jealous bitch.

Jo   I never said anything!

Lucy   Bet yer 'ant been fucked in yonks, 'ave yer?

Jo   What? . . . F'Chrissakes, he's not an idiot, Lucy, he's –

Lucy   Buttin' in. Ruin' everythin'. Mum, Nikki, me –
Think yer fuckin' Gandhi or somert.

Jo   That's enough.

Lucy   Think yer fuckin' Gandhi, keep us for yersen. Yeah,
must be 'ard at your age. Waitin' to die like that. Buried
alive. (*Pause.*) Buried alive! Crap! Rotten fuckin' crap!

Jo   Yeah, well wait till they catch sight o'you, dear. Dirt
like you with . . . with death written all over yer.

Lucy   Yeah?

Jo   Whore. Waste o'fuckin' space –

Lucy   Arrrr.

Jo   You and yer docile bloody sister! All I've done, all the
time I've wasted.

Lucy   Come on –

Jo   Not worth the ground she walked upon, neither of yer,
pair o' bloody –

Lucy *yanks* **Jo***'s glasses and throws them.*

Lucy   Makes us even then dunt it, love?

Jo *tries to move,* **Lucy** *stops her.*

Lucy   'Bout all yer good for.

Lucy *grabs* **Jo** *by the head and kisses her.* **Jo** *struggles.* **Lucy** *bites*
Jo*'s lip.* **Jo** *screams.*

Lucy   Should put yer in a zoo lookin' like that. Pig.

Jo   Lucy, please, I can't see a –

Lucy   Pig!

She slaps **Jo**.

Mek me sick just lookin' at yer, pig.

She slaps **Jo** *repeatedly across the face. The slaps turn into blows with her fist.*

Lucy (*as she strikes*)   Pig, pig, pig, pig, pig, pig. Last f'you, pig! Last f'you!

Lucy *grabs* **Jo** *and pushes her to the ground.*

Blackout.

Scene Six

Three weeks later. Day.

Lucy *in bed.*
Darren *sits on the edge, getting dressed.*

Lucy   Did 'urt a bit.

Darren   Should o'said somert then, shunt yer?

Pause.

Lucy   Thought yer liked it.

Darren   Worried it'll bruise?

Lucy   Thought yer liked it.

Darren   I did. Shuddup about it, will yer?

Pause.

Lucy   Yer will come back, won't yer?

Darren   'Course.

Lucy   Not just sayin' that.

Darren   No.

Lucy   People say things, see?

Darren   Not me.

Lucy   That's what I like about you.

Pause.

Gettin' disability allowance now. What wi'me back n'that.

Darren   Oh. That's 'andy.

Lucy   Tell 'em anythin', me. Talk me way out of owt.
Never change, do I?

Pause.

Darren   Whose was it then?

Pause.
Lucy *kisses* **Darren**.

Darren   Whose was it?

Lucy *kisses* **Darren**.
Pause.

Darren   Look. I know it's not really your thing, but . . .

*He reaches into his jeans pocket and pulls out a Pentecostal Church
pamphlet, gives it to* **Lucy**.

When yer've got time. When yer've got a day free. Give us a
ring. We're all friends. Think yer'll be surprised.

Pause.

Lucy   Yer will come back though, won't yer, Darren? Yer
will come back? Say yer'll come back. Come back.

Lights fade.

Scene Seven.

Night. Late December.

The flat is practically bare. The curtains are open. Two large heavy bin bags on the bed. **Lucy** *fills up the binbags with her junk.* **Nikki** *stands in the open doorway.*

Lucy Thought yer'd bin abducted. Sucked up on a flyin' saucer or somert.

Nikki What d'yer want, Luce?

Lucy Oh, cheer up, yer ninny, I'm only jokin'. D'yer want a cup o'tea?

Nikki No ta.

Lucy Are you alright? Yer don't look alright.

Nikki Bin up since five this mornin'.

Lucy Arrr. Mek a brew if yer want. Stood there like a bloody tent peg, sit down.

Nikki I've gotta get back.

Lucy Five minutes int gonna hurt yer. Go on.

Nikki 'Ad to tek 'er round the neighbours, Luce. They're not 'appy about it neither. Bad enough 'er cryin' mornin', noon n'night keepin' the whole street up without me dumpin' 'er on total strangers n'all. It's not fair, Luce. She won't stop.

Lucy Med up me mind, Nik.

Nikki Don't give a fuck, d'yer?

Lucy Alright, alright, don't get yer knickers in a twist. 'Ant even told yer yet.

Nikki What?

Lucy Was thinkin' about robbin' the Chinky. (*Pause.*) I'm jokin'. God, can't yer take a joke no more?

Nikki Not when it comes out o'your mouth, no.

Lucy Well, yer'll 'ave to get used to it, sis. I'm comin' 'ome.

Nikki   What?

Lucy   Mad innit. Gran was right. Best thing really.
Thought yer'd be surprised. Just decided, like. Be great,
won't it? Just like the old days.

Nikki   And that's why yer dragged me over 'ere, is it?

Lucy   Yeah. 'Elp us carry me stuff, can't yer?

Nikki   You are jokin' aren't yer?

Lucy   Free country. Do what I like. Get the bus can't we?

Nikki   You're not right. You need a doctor.

Lucy   Doctor Who. 'Ere, d'yer like me trainers? Cost a
bomb, like. Whole bloody giro. Typical. Typical me. Go
n'treat mesen n'I leave meself skint. Good though, aren't
they? Adidas. Go wi'me socks, don't they? Green. Like little
Christmas trees.

Nikki (*to herself*)   Don't bloody need this.

Lucy   Long as I keep 'em clean.

Nikki   You must think I'm mad.

Lucy   What?

Gonzo *enters, holding a crappy microwave in his arms. He kicks the
front door open.*

Gonzo   Fucksake! Killer those stairs, innit?

He dumps the microwave down.

'Ere, don't move, alright? Jocy's doin' 'er nut.

Gonzo *exits.*
Pause.
Lucy *inspects the microwave.*

Lucy   Ooh. That's nice, int it? Go well in the kitchen that.
Yer still got that calendar with all the kittens on it? Am
serious, Nik.

Nikki   Yeah.

Lucy   Start again like. The two of us.

Nikki   In yer fuckin' dreams we will.

Lucy   Oh, come on, don't be like that.

Nikki   After what you did to Gran? After you put 'er in a fuckin' . . . ?!

Lucy   Since when? No. No, yer wrong, I . . .

Nikki   Should lock you up.

Lucy   Never touched 'er!

Nikki   Little bitch.

Lucy   I never touched 'er! Please, Nikki. Come on, let's not fight, not now. Sure yer don't want a cup o'tea?

Nikki   She's not comin' back, Luce.

Lucy   Eh?

Nikki   They're gonna put 'er in an 'ome.

Lucy   No they're not.

Nikki   She can 'ardly even talk straight! Whole right side of 'er . . . 'Cause o'you.

Lucy   Naow.

Nikki   Cunt 'ardly recognise 'er at first. Drinkin' out this little plastic cup they give 'er. Funnel on side, like. Wipin' 'er mouth every two seconds. And them, wheelin' 'er down ward like an astronaut forra bath. Can't even go the bog wi'out some – Are you smilin'?

Lucy   Don't be stupid.

Nikki   Think it's fuckin' funny?

Lucy   No!

Nikki   All she ever does is ask about you n'all. N'there's me stood like . . . like I'm invisible or somert, 'avin' to lie on your be'alf.

Lucy   Never asked yer to.

Nikki   Lucky she never pressed no charges.

Lucy   I won't bother you or owt.

Nikki   What?

Lucy   Just stay in me room if yer want.

Nikki   Jesus Christ, are you fuckin' deaf?

Lucy   I'll 'elp with the washin'-up n'that.

Nikki   What, while I look after the baby?

Lucy   No.

Nikki   S'ppose we'll draw up a rota then, yeah?

Lucy   Whatever.

Nikki   Long as you're 'appy.

Lucy   Yeah. All of us. Simple, int it?

Nikki   Yeah.

Lucy   Yeah. Get a job or somert.

Nikki   What? Finally goin' on game, are yer? 'Bout all yer bloody good for.

Pause.

Well. It's true, innit?

Lucy   No, I mean it, Nikki. I'll go college or somert. Promise.

Nikki   Look . . .

Lucy   Cross me 'eart, Nik.

Nikki   It's too late anyway, Luce.

Pause.

Movin' in wi'Brendan, aren't I? 'Im n'is dad. Said they'd put us up forra bit while I . . .

Lucy   Since when?

Nikki   F'fucksake, Luce . . .

Lucy   Yer can't do that!

Nikki   I'm doin' it.

Lucy   Yer can't.

Nikki   Got no other choice, 'ave I?

Lucy   Yes you 'ave.

Nikki   I can barely afford the rent, Luce.

Lucy   We'll pay it together, won't we?

Nikki   Don't be stupid.

Lucy   I'll get a job.

Nikki   Yer livin' in a dream world!

Pause.

There's room there, there's space, Luce. Goin' mad back there, on me own, bloody social knockin' on the door every five seconds, it's . . . It's too much. I can't handle it no more, look at me! I fuckin' hate you. What you've done to me, it's not fair! You n'yer fuckin' baby. Feel like flushin' it down the bog sometimes.

Pause.

Surprised you even know 'er name.

Pause.

Lucy   She alright?

Nikki   Since when 'ave you bin bothered? Yeah. Yeah, she's . . . Over 'er cold anyway.

Lucy   Oh. Well, that's good.

Nikki   Gonna tek 'er to Whirlow Farm next week. Tek t'see the cows n'that. Brendan's gonna drive us there at the weekend. Come along if yer want.

Lucy   Went there wi'school once.

Pause.

Be good though, wunt it?

Nikki   Eh?

Lucy   Me n'you. Be good. Be like that song. (*Pause, signals to the bags.*) Fuckin' psycho, me, aren't I? Eh? Fuckin' psycho bird.

Pause.

D'yer love 'im?

Nikki   Yeah? (*Pause.*) Yeah. When 'e's not talkin' shit. (*Pause.*) Once in a blue moon.

Pause.

Lucy   Might just go the pictures anyway. There's a cinema in Barnsley, 'ave a fag n'everythin'.

Nikki   'Ant bin the pictures in ages.

Lucy   No. Me neither. Bit o'freedom, innit?

Nikki   Yeah.

Pause.

Should 'ave a bath.

Lucy   'Ow come like?

Nikki   'Cause yer stink?

Lucy   No I don't.

Nikki   Yer bloody do n'all.

Nikki *gets up, exits into the bathroom.*

Lucy *sits motionless.*
The bath taps are turned on, offstage.

Lucy   Yerra good girl, Nikki!

Nikki (*off*)   Eh?

Pause.

Nikki *re-enters, shutting the door behind her.*

Nikki   What yer say?

Gonzo *enters, quickly, out of breath.*

Gonzo   Honestly, Luce, these people are fuckin'
scumbags. (*Pause.*) Oh, alright. This a mate o'yours, is it?

Nikki   We're sisters.

Gonzo   Not interruptin' owt, am I?

Pause.

Tek that as a no then, yeah? 'Ere . . . (*Taps the roof of the
microwave.*) . . . what d'yer think? Same bloke gi'us the telly.

Lucy   Yeah.

Gonzo   Dial's a bit wonky like.

Nikki (*to Lucy*)   Listen, are you gonna be OK?

Gonzo   Name's Gonzo, by the way.

He extends his hand. **Nikki** *freezes.*
Pause.

Gonzo   I'm not a bloody leper or nothin'.

Nikki   That's 'im, innit?

Gonzo   What? (*To* **Lucy**.) She a bit . . . ? (*Pause.*) Fuck me,
yer ever see that film, *Night of the Livin' Dead*?

Gonzo *pulls a can of Coke out of his jacket and lights a fag.*

Nikki   'Ere. Don't forget yer bath, eh?

Lucy   Thanks.

Nikki   I'll pop round in a day or two.

Lucy   Yeah.

Gonzo   Good t'meet yer, yeah?

Nikki *exits.*

Gonzo   Yeah, and you. Bloody 'ell, barrel o'laughs that
one, int she?

*He takes rocks, pipe, etc., out of his jacket and starts building a
crackpipe.*

Can't stay long meself actually, fuckin' . . . People lettin' me
down, yer know? Fuckin' schmeigals. Make me wanna . . .
blow up, star. Just 'avin' t'smell 'em, it's like . . . Words can't
describe it, yer know? Dogshit all oer landin'. Needles
everywhere, fuckin' . . . Three 'en'em wi'this Greek bird.
Fuck knows 'ow she got mixed up wi'them. S'pposed t'be
studyin' or somert. Sat in corner wi'the shakes like. Breaks
yer 'eart. And them all fuckin' mouth. Givin' off like fuckin'
Oasis, tryin' t'scam us like I'm some sort o'dial-a-fuckin'-
skag. Burnin' up me wallet, star. Me, a grown man. Wife
n'kid t'support.

Pause. He realises what he's said.

Can keep that.

Pause.
He lights and smokes his pipe.
Long pause.

'Ere. Yer don't mind, do yer?

Lucy   What?

Gonzo *offers the pipe to* **Lucy.**

Gonzo   Look like yer could do with it.

Lucy *hesitates.*

Gonzo   Well, go on. Pack up yer troubles.

Gonzo *passes* **Lucy** *the pipe.* **Lucy** *smokes.*
Long pause.
Lucy *and* **Gonzo** *sit sharing the pipe.*

Gonzo   Lot more where that came from n'all.

Pause.

Like yer trainers.

Lucy   D'yer?

Gonzo   Yeah. Good colour n'that. They new?

Pause.
Gonzo *starts loading another pipe.*

Lucy   Love me trainers me.

Gonzo   Mind if I bring a mate o'mine round next time.

Lucy   Who?

Gonzo   Mate o'mine. I were tellin' 'im about you today. Wants to meet yer like. Good bloke actually. (*Pause.*) That alright?

Lucy   Yeah? 'Course.

Gonzo   You on the Pill?

Lucy   Eh?

Gonzo   No, just . . . Yer know?

Pause.

Lucy   Look after mesen, can't I?

Pause.

Gonzo   That's alright then. Long as yer know.

Lucy   My life.

Pause.

Gonzo Where've yer bin anyway? Bin knockin' all day.

Lucy Eh?

Gonzo Yer goin' somewhere? What's wi'all the luggage?

Lucy Nothin'. Just thought.

Gonzo What?

Lucy Went round Darren's earlier.

Gonzo 'Oo?

Lucy Weren't in anyway. Just lookin' through window. For ages like. Livin' room. Books. Plants. Carpet. Big leather sofa n'that. Pictures on walls. (*Pause.*) Must o'been out to a restaurant or somert. Fuckin' theatre. Sort o'thing they'd do innit? (*Pause.*) Just stood there. Ages like. Kept tellin' meself to move, but . . . (*Pause.*) They've got this fireplace, right? Coal. Fake fuckin' coal. (*Pause.*) Felt like pissin' on it.

Gonzo 'Ere.

He passes the pipe to **Lucy**.

Joan of bloody Arc.

Lucy *takes the pipe and smokes.*

Long pause.

Gonzo 'Av t'get off soon. Jocy's bought this iguana like. Scary fuckin' thing. Got a tub full o'locusts in the car. (*Pause.*) That is what they eat, int it?

Lucy Got to eat somert.

She passes the pipe to **Gonzo**, *who smokes.*
Pause.
She rests.
Pause.

Got to eat somert. (*Pause. Chuckles.*) Locusts. (*Pause. Sighs.*) Oh. Fuck it.

Gonzo *finishes the pipe, sits back.*
Pause.

Lucy   Don't s'ppose yer fancy a game o' . . . ? Oh, yeah.
Lizard. Forgot.

Pause.
She stares at **Gonzo***.*

Professor Plum.

Gonzo   What?

Lucy *tenderly touches* **Gonzo***'s nose.*
Gonzo *pretends to hit her,* **Lucy** *flinches.*
Long pause.
Lucy *gets up and walks to the window.*

Gonzo   Sounds nice that place.

Lucy *peers out of the window.*

Lucy   Oh. It's snowin', look.

Pause.
She moves to **Gonzo***.*

Look. Look, Gonz.

No response. **Lucy** *sits back down.*

Gonzo   Right.

He slowly sits up, pulling on his jacket.

That's it. I'm done. Yer gonna be alright? (*Pause.*) Yeah,
well . . .

He stands – headrush. He nearly stumbles over.

Oooh, fuck me. Fuckin' 'eadrush.

Lucy (*laughs*)   Eh?

Gonzo (*laughs*)   Jesus. Look at 'em.

Gonzo *starts clapping the space in front of him, as though killing
flies.* **Lucy** *laughs.*

Lucy   Gonzo.

Gonzo   Little bastards. Yer ever get that? Like gold dust or somert. Microscopic angels.

He claps some more, then stops.

Gonzo   That's 'ow I know there's a Great Spirit like.

Lucy   What?

Gonzo   Great Spirit. Separate realities n'that. Carlos Castaneda. I'll lend you a book about it, if yer want. Tells yer how t'control yer dreams n'that. Consciously like. Shape shift. Them angels then? Messages from the other side. T'remind yer.

Lucy   Of what?

Gonzo   What's what, star, what's what. Why we're 'ere, yer know? Whole bloody point of it all. We're plannin' on goin' Mexico, like. Me n'Joce. Gonna try out some o'that peyote. Fly through clouds, like . . . (*Poses.*) Da-da-da-daaaah!

Lucy   Gi'us a kiss.

Gonzo   Eh?

Lucy   Gi'us a kiss.

Gonzo   And then what? I know what you're like.

Lucy   Go on.

Gonzo   I'm done wi'that remember?

Pause.

'Ere.

He digs in his pocket and pulls out two rocks wrapped in cling film.

So's yer don't get too bored.

He gives the rocks to **Lucy**.

Yeah?

Gonzo *kisses* **Lucy**.
Pause.

Lucy   Men.

Gonzo   What?

Lucy   Never give up, d'yer?

Pause.
Lucy *stares into space.*
Gonzo *gathers his things together – mobile phone, keys, etc.*

Lucy   Go the pictures.

Pause.

Gonzo   I'll pop round tomorrow, alright? (*Pause.*) Get that thing plugged in. Bit of a sesh. Just three of us, like, yeah? I mean . . . Yer not got owt planned 'ave yer? Yer'll still be 'ere, won't yer? Money t'be made.

Pause.

Oh, f'fucksake, Luce, cheer up.

Gonzo *exits.*
Long pause.
Sigh.

Lucy *eyes the microwave. She presses the button which opens the door, it 'bings'. She shuts the door. She opens it again, 'bing'.*

Pause.

Lucy *exits into the bathroom. Turns the taps off.*

Lucy *re-enters, shutting the bathroom door.*

Lucy *sits. She takes the crackpipe, cleans the gauze. She stops.*

Lucy *moves to the tape recorder. She takes the cassette out, turns it over and presses play: Bob Marley.*

Lucy *stands, moves, sits, listens.*

Pause.

Lucy *moves to the tape recorder, stops the tape. She takes the tape out and puts it in its box.*

Pause.

Lucy *sits. Stares into space.*

Pause.

Lucy *picks up the crackpipe, checks the gauze. She stops.*

Pause.

Lucy *rubs her head in her hands, wipes away the tears, sniffles. She hesitates, stops, hesitates, stops.*

Lucy *gets up, moves to the window, opens the curtains.*

Snow is falling.

Lucy *sits on the bed, stares out of the window, transfixed.*

Pause.

Lucy *scratches her head.*

Lights fade.